# PRAISE FOR *SERVICE TO C...*

"Nathan Gould takes readers throu... hardships he faced in war, law enforce... that followed. It's an in-depth story of de... ...ne made career decisions that sunk him deeper and deeper into depression. This book will most certainly resonate with others like myself who have experienced PTSD from active combat or police work.

"PTSD is not something new. We first started hearing about it after WWI when doctors described it as being shell shocked. Nathan Gould's journey gives us a more modern-day look into PTSD as we identify just how widespread PTSD is among those who have served in war and among law enforcement. Nathan lays it all on the line: his life before, during, and after active combat when he decides to work in police work. The PTSD that followed his many traumatic experiences is palpable through his excellent storytelling. As someone who has experienced PTSD, and had to stop sleeping in the same bed with my wife because of violent outbursts in my sleep, I found this book to be an excellent example of just how scary life can become following such traumatic experiences. This is a must-read for young and old alike."

—**Jackie Hubbard,** Rocky Mount Police Department twenty-six years, Narcotics Officer, Chief Investigator

"Nathan Gould's book is a relatively short autobiographical narrative of a combat veteran's experience in Iraq, and transitioning home again. Gould's narrative is both raw and powerful, taking the reader through basic training to his interactions with Army culture and politics, to his combat experiences, and back again. Gould does not spare details in this account, and provides helpful photographs throughout the book. What is portrayed to the reader is a convincing indictment of a humiliating, traumatizing, and dehumanizing military culture, and the difficulties of regaining one's personhood and personal relationships after transitioning back to civilian life.

The book ends with a glimmer of hope and a pathway forward. Gould's account may provide hope and understanding to other combat veterans who have felt that they have lost themselves and are alone in their despair. The book will also be of interest to anyone who is curious about military culture and the development of PTSD. After reading this book, it is difficult not to be convinced regarding the need to change that culture."

—**Robert J. Gregory**, MD, Professor of Psychiatry, Upstate Medical University, Director, Psychiatry High Risk Program

"Before reading *Service to Civilian: A Journey Through PTSD*, I'd already spent many hours researching PTSD. I am close to a couple people that personally have PTSD. I, however, not having had any comparable traumatic life experiences, placed PTSD in the incorrect categories of 'mind over matter, get over it' or 'convenient way to get benefits' or 'like kids diagnosed with ADHD, take meds to solve the problem.' I did not give it the proper weight and relegated it to a problem that could probably be tackled with good counseling.

"*Service to Civilian: A Journey Through PTSD* opened my eyes to the gravity of the experiences and mental toll that happens during active duty military service and in police work. I have a greater understanding and compassion for those that have PTSD and increased awe for the sacrifice of those who wear the uniforms. *Service to Civilian: A Journey Through PTSD* does not spotlight PTSD; rather it focuses in on the life and experiences that led to PTSD. This book is for those who want to get into the head of someone who is diagnosed with PTSD. I am thankful for Nathan's vulnerability and opening up his life to everyone. That is a very humbling and courageous thing to do. Lastly, *Service to Civilian: A Journey Through PTSD* is not a bunch of 'do this and you're better.' It's a view of how Nathan has struggled and how he has been able to function with PTSD and give hope to those that don't think they can."

—**Dana Parker**, Licensed Realtor, Lifelong Friend

"This book is for anyone who has faced loss. Grief comes in many different ways. When it involves tragedy, the survivors sometimes suffer with PTSD. I know this firsthand as I have suffered and overcome PTSD. You can be blindsided at any moment, always facing uncontrollable emotions, and trying to dig yourself out of the depths of depression.

"This transparent journey Nathan shares will encourage you to begin your own healing process. God sees the scars on the outside and inside of the wars we face, either on the battlefield or within our families.

"I personally want to thank Nathan for his service to our country. This was such a reminder to me that my freedom is due to the bravery of everyone that serves in the military. I pray God bless each man and woman that is suffering from trauma and that He will heal them physically, mentally and spiritually."

—**Julie Kemp**, Author of *Faith Has Its Reasons* and *Highway to Heaven*, www.faithhasitsreasons.com

"As a psychotherapist for fifteen years specializing in suicide, I know many people struggle to recall aspects of their trauma and struggle even more to talk about it. People consider suicide often when they feel they have no other option, and Nathan humbly shares that experience and encourages others that there is a way out. In a time when our servicemen and first responders are demoralized in our culture, my hope is that this book will start to revitalize and redeem a broken military and police culture. I also hope it encourages those suffering in silence to seek hope, help, and healing. Every life has dignity, worth, and value."

—**Abigail Riggall**, LCSW-R, Assistant Director High Risk Program, Assistant Professor, Department of Psychiatry, SUNY Upstate Medical University

*Service to Civilian: A Journey Through PTSD*

by Nathan Gould

ISBN 978-1-64663-330-2

Published by

**koehlerbooks**™

3705 Shore Drive
Virginia Beach, VA 23455
800-435-4811
www.koehlerbooks.com

# SERVICE
## TO CIVILIAN

### A JOURNEY THROUGH PTSD

## NATHAN GOULD

VIRGINIA BEACH

CAPE CHARLES

# TABLE OF CONTENTS

# DEDICATION

To all the selfless men and women of the armed services, all first responders, and any form of law enforcement, foreign or domestic: I salute you. You are the backbone of this country's greatness. To all of you who feel like the system has failed you and you have slipped through the cracks of legality, I urge you: press on. Do not give up. There is light at the end of the tunnel, so keep going. To those who have fallen on hard times and have lost all hope and might even be contemplating suicide: I've been there. Join my journey in these pages and you will be offered better alternative options. To my wife Rianne, who has stood with me through thick and thin: I couldn't have done it without you, babe! To my many counselors, pastors, doctors, mentors, friends, and family: I love you all! You've all individually helped guide me toward my own mental, physical, and spiritual wholeness. You are the best!

*Be strong and courageous. Do not be afraid or terrified because of them, for the Lord your God goes with you; he will never leave you nor forsake you.*
—Deuteronomy 31:6 (NIV)

# DISCLAIMER

The stories in this book reflect the author's best recollection of events. Some names, locations, and identifying characteristics have been changed to protect the privacy of those depicted. Dialogue has been recreated from memory. The stories herein are not intended to hurt any of the people portrayed but instead bring to the light how the author developed the mental illness of PTSD and how other similar illnesses develop.

# FORWARD OF
# FORGIVENESS

**FIRST, I WOULD LIKE TO** start by saying that what I'm about to tell you is no one's fault. But there are people who made decisions that affected the lives of others, and no one is perfect. For my part, I forgive anyone who did or may have wronged me or anyone in my care. Whether they knew what they were doing or not, I forgive them. In turn, I also ask for forgiveness from those I have wronged, whether I knew what I was doing or not. I am truly sorry. In these pages I will unfold a story that may paint some people in a bad light. I am not intending to hurt or harm them. It is all to show how and why I developed post-traumatic stress disorder, commonly known as PTSD.

I also would like to note that this book is about my journey through PTSD; it is not everyone's journey, but I hope it gives you insight into how PTSD develops and some constructive avenues toward regaining wholeness mentally, physically, and spiritually. This PTSD epidemic attacks your core values, poisons the best parts of who you are, and is a never-ending nightmare you just can't seem to wake up from. If this sounds like you, I encourage you to seek help before the inevitable thoughts of suicide begin to overtake your mind as the only way of escape! Brother or sister, I do not know you, and you have no reason to trust me right now, but maybe after you read this account of part of my life, you will be convinced to embark on one of the hardest missions you will ever endure: the road to recovery. It is not for the faint of heart! The freedom from guilt/sin/shame or whatever is haunting you, is worth the pain of reliving your worst real nightmare. So, let's start where all stories start, at the very beginning.

# CHRISTIAN UPBRINGING

**HERE'S A LITTLE BIT OF** my background and where I come from, just to get you started. I was brought up in a Christian home in upstate New York. My family and I believed, and still believe, that you should treat others as you would like to be treated. I still believe that I need to show others love like Jesus has shown me, in that he gave up his life for you and for me, even though we continue to sin. I do not believe in killing, lying, cheating, coveting, taking the Lord's name in vain, and follow the rest of the Ten Commandments to the best of my ability. We went to church every time the doors were open, it seemed. We only listened to Christian radio programs. We rarely watched TV and when we did, it was the Disney Sunday night movie that my father had taped on the VCR to watch later. There was no alcohol or drug use in our house. We learned not to swear, because if we did our mouths were washed out with soap or we had to eat a full raw onion with only water to wash it down. On top of that, we would have to write a passage from the Bible for punishment and memorization. During my freshman year of high school, my parents decided to homeschool us because the school system was too secular, and they wanted our minds not to be tainted by society's evolutionary thought and other-worldly ways. During this time my siblings and I underwent intense psychological attacks, mainly from our mother.

When I was about five years-old my mother wished to teach me that the stove is hot. It was one of those electric stoves with the coils that turned red when they were hot. My mother held me in her arms and told me that the stove was hot, and she did not want me to touch it ever and then she proceeded to take my small hand and to place it on the hot coils. Before she could, I pleaded and cried that she wouldn't make me do it and that I believed her that it was hot and I would not ever touch it, but I got burned that day.

Another time, I remember running away from my mother because I was going to get a licking for something I did not do. I remember a mixture of fear, righteous anger, and a not-caring-anymore attitude. I ran out of our yard, through the neighbors' yards and into some brambles, cutting up my legs. I could've easily gone around the briars, but the pain made me feel better in a weird way. After running across a local street and then another open property, I came to a hill. The rocky mound used to be part of an old bridge of stone that crossed over the Cayuga outlet that ran through our small town. It was like a small tower that rose up on the edge of what we called *the outlet* that eventually ran into the Seneca river. As I stood upon this precipice, I contemplated what I would do next. I thought about jumping. I told myself, as I was only about twenty feet up, that I would just break a leg or get hurt and just be mad. So I didn't jump. I just sat there crying. After what seemed like hours and I had cried all I could, I decided to walk home. It was dark when I got home, but I did not go in. Instead I went to a window and looked in to see my family at the dinner table eating. It did not look like anyone noticed I was not there. I waited until well after they were done to go inside, straight to my room, and go to bed. In the morning no one asked me where I was the previous evening. I don't remember ever talking about any of it. It was just forgotten.

Another instance I remember was after I got my driver's license as a teenager. My mother would have me drive every possible time we were in the car together. One of those times, we were heading to Wednesday night church in Syracuse, New York and my best friend was in the backseat. We were listening to our Christian radio station or a Christian cassette tape. Suddenly my mother turned off the radio without saying anything. I waited a few moments and then I turned it back on without saying anything. And just as quickly, without saying a word, my mother slapped me across the face as I was driving and turned off the radio again. She did it right in front of my best friend. For another hour we drove to church without speaking a word to one another and then again, after church was over, we drove home in complete silence.

This is just a small window into my upbringing. I only share this to give you an understanding of the psychological abuse which I believe also made me vulnerable to PTSD later on in life.

# COLLEGE, MARRIAGE, AND THE ARMY

**AFTER COMPLETING MY HOMESCHOOL EDUCATION,** I was really in a very psychologically beaten-down state of mind. I could not wait to get out of the house and be on my own somewhere, anywhere; it didn't matter. When I found out that one of my best friends was going to Eastern Nazarene College, I decided I wanted to go there, too. I did not think about it; I did not care about the details; I just wanted to go. My mother wanted me to go to a Jewish school somewhere between Rochester and Buffalo, New York. I felt like this was just another way for her to attempt to control me by determining my next major life decision. Thank God that didn't happen because I wanted nothing more than to get away from her.

I went to college with no direction and no real reason to go, other than to get away from home. I had normal struggles at school, including my first mental breakdown, for which I sought counseling. By my junior year I was in a pretty good place; I had a plan, and I was taking my time to graduate. But the cost of school was getting real!

Also during this year, I met and started dating Rianne Henning. By the end of my junior year and her freshman year, we were already thinking about getting married and had purchased rings. At this point, she decided to move back to North Carolina on very short notice, so the plans I had to graduate in my own timeframe kind of went out the window. All of a sudden, I found out she was moving back to North Carolina and we had not even discussed it. I proposed to her one evening down at Wollaston Beach in Quincy, Massachusetts. The next day I helped her father pack up the U-Haul with all of her things and they left for North Carolina. Shortly after that, I gave my two weeks-notice at my job and followed her down there.

I did not have a degree and I did not know anyone in North Carolina, except for Rianne's family, so I began to work with her father in his carpet cleaning business. We did not see eye to eye, and just before Rianne and I were married on July 20, 2002, I quit cleaning carpets with her father. I began working for FedEx and when that didn't work out, I became a delivery driver for Papa John's Pizza. Soon my young wife and I found ourselves not being able to afford our apartment, and we moved in with her mother, into the same room she grew up in. I felt like an utter failure and I dreamed at night how I could get out of this situation. A friend of mine who was in the National Guard suggested that I should look into joining the military. The next thing I knew, I was down in Charlotte talking to an Army recruiter and my beautiful wife and I made one of the hardest decisions we have ever made together: I joined the Army. I did not join for my country. I did not join because of 9/11. I did not join because it was something I wanted to do; I joined purely to pay off college debt and because we felt trapped in our current situation.

So there you have it, a short synopsis of how and why I joined the military. Now I invite you to go on my military journey with me, which I believe will give you further evidence of how and why PTSD develops.

# CHAPTER 1: BASIC TRAINING

**LEAVING FOR BASIC TRAINING WAS** super scary. I was going into the unknown. Boot camp would introduce me to the army and teach me how to be a soldier, which I knew nothing about. I remember riding some type of charter bus with a whole bunch of other recruits all the way to Fort Leonard Wood, Missouri. To say the least, I had anxiety and did not sleep the whole trip and pretty much white-knuckled the seat in front of me. There's not too much I want to say about basic training. Yes, it was challenging. It was also an awesome time and I learned a lot, and I was in the best physical condition of my life. There are a couple of underlying military values that begin in basic training and are built upon later in garrison. Although these values are quite helpful on the battlefield, they also are the beginnings of a subtle PTSD journey. One of these core values is basically to never give up, and with every drill, every exercise, every moment, this is squeezed into your brain. And an even greater core value, is this *Army of One* concept, the idea of completing the mission no matter the cost, even if you're the only one left. Drill sergeants are great at scare tactics. They have to build soldiers, and they only have a certain timeframe to do it in. It is a well-oiled machine. It has great results. The first mission is to graduate basic training. Drill sergeants let you know in the very beginning and all throughout training that you will have to get what they call *recycled* if you are a *No Go.* Recycling is the most feared punishment in basic training because it means that if you do not complete the tasks according to standards, you will be sent back to the beginning with a new company, in a new group of recruits. No one wants to spend more time in basic training, so mentally you know you have no choice; you cannot fail or you'll have to go back to the beginning and do it until you do it right. You don't want to be a No Go. There are obvious things that will send you back to the beginning, like getting hurt or not qualifying on your M-16. And the drill sergeants would say something like this, "Hey, you can go to sick call if you want, but if you get hospitalized, you will definitely get recycled, we don't care what you do! It's your choice, privates!"

I remember two specific instances when I should have gone to sick call, but I didn't because I did not want to get recycled. Once was when I got frostbite during our field training exercise in January on my big left toe. The other time I should have gone was just before Thanksgiving when we were allowed to go home for two weeks on what they called *Exodus,* where the Army shuts down all of its training schools to let the drill sergeants and instructors have a break during the holidays. At the time, we were training in cold weather and it had been raining so we stayed in wet and cold uniforms. Also, we slept in the barracks with the heat on high and the windows wide open and my bunk was directly in front of the open window. I knew I was sick, but I refused to go to sick call. Even if the drill instructors knew you were sick, they would not make you go—it was your decision. When we were released to go on our Exodus, I got home and was immediately admitted into the hospital where they

*Christmas (Exodus) break from Basic Training 2003.*

treated me for double pneumonia. Within two weeks I went back to basic training and finished up.

So those are the two military core values I took from basic training: never give up or never quit and if you are hurt, ignore it. And then there are the military catch phrases everyone learns, like, *I hate it for you, privates!* or *drink water; drive on!* Those basically acknowledge that the situation sucks—or is going to. *Take a knee; face out; pull security* means to stay on guard while we figure out what we're doing. And my favorite phrase is, *that's the three p's, privates: piss poor planning!* That is code for saying that the higher-ups have no clue what they're doing.

# CHAPTER 2: FORT CAMPBELL, KENTUCKY

**MY FIRST DUTY STATION WAS** at Fort Campbell, Kentucky, the home of the 101st Airborne Air Assault Screaming Eagles (*Hooah!*). The 101st is a specialized modular light infantry division of the US Army that is trained for air assault operations. My time at Fort Campbell enhanced the *Army of One* mentality to keep going, finish the mission, and don't seek help. Whereas basic training broke you down in order to build you up and make you better, life in garrison broke you down for fun—also known as hazing. At least this was my experience. Before I left basic training, I could almost get a perfect score of 300+ on my physical training (PT) tests. During my time spent at Fort Campbell, originally 3rd Brigade, 326th C Company Zone, my physical health declined. We did a twelve-mile march with fully loaded rucksacks, called a *ruck march* at least once a month, and if you hadn't passed Air Assault School yet, you did it every week. We ran so much I dropped from B running group to C group. Every new soldier got hazed, it was just what they did. There was normal hazing that everybody got, like being demeaned by any non-commissioned officer (NCO) in the unit all day long, to include while you were working or doing PT. Then there was the extreme hazing that only certain individuals received, mostly if they screwed up on something. You didn't want to be that guy because that hazing often lasted the whole time they were in the unit, horrible!

One day I had an early dental appointment—simple right? Nope, I was late to the appointment by a few minutes. That was considered a *missed movement*, so they sent me to tell my superiors that I missed the appointment. It just so happened that the same day there was a brigade formation for something and when I got back to the unit only a few NCOs were there. The NCO in charge (NCOIC) put me on a lawnmower and told me to mow the lawns until everyone was back. No biggie, so I mowed the lawn for a few hours. When the unit got finished with the brigade formation, they came back to our company area and immediately we were all put into a company formation while 1st Sgt. Siciliano pissed and moaned about how they fidgeted during the brigade formation. It had been a very hot day, and everyone had been squirming while standing in the sun at the *attention* position for a dumb formation for about two hours. Although I had not been in the brigade formation, I had also been in the sun for two hours while mowing lawns. None of us had been given any water and were now forced to stand in another stupid formation soaking up the sun, great! In this formation, I and at least one or two other soldiers began to feel lightheaded. To avoid passing out I took a knee. I was supposed to be standing in the *parade rest* position with my feet apart and my hands clasped behind my back, listening to First Sgt. Siciliano rant and rave. First Sgt. Siciliano took this personally and demanded that I immediately stand up, and I did for a few seconds before going back down to a knee. Then he demanded others to lift me up, and when they did, I passed out. So began my extreme hazing. My immediate supervisor, Sgt. Macon, was tasked to correct my insubordination. That afternoon and for the coming months I always had to have a full canteen of water on me *dummy corded* to my wrist. It really wasn't carrying the canteen that got to me, it was the unnecessary verbal abuse that constantly spewed out of his mouth. At the time I developed an extreme hatred toward him. This was during 2004 and I was twenty-seven years old, married, and I did not need to be treated as a child. He wasn't that much older than me, and in fact we might've been the same age. I won't lie, I fantasized about killing him often during those months.

Never seek help! This was basically the mantra of our unit. If you wanted to go to sick call, you would get the dirtiest looks and you would be verbally abused and hazed for it. If you were hurt, you'd really better be badly hurt or else you would never live it down. Our unit was renowned for this type of behavior and got a reputation for being badasses because of it. So, we pretty much took the *never give up* attitude to the extreme. I know it was physically damaging to my body, but my experience with hazing taught me to never seek help or admit I was in pain or had any type of problem; it was always "I'm good." I remember going on ruck marches until all my joints were hurting. On ruck marches we were in *full battle rattle*, where we wore our inceptor body armor (IBA), Kevlar, fighting load carrier (FLC) vest, thirty-five pound ruck, etc. and carried our *combat loaded* weapon as well as all the extra ammunition I would actually carry during a combat mission. I could barely lift my legs because my hips did not want to move and there was no comfortable position for my pack or for my weapon; it was just a suck fest. I remember putting my ruck down after completing the five-hour march and realizing that circulation had been cut off to my arms for a long time. The rucksack most likely had been pinching my nerves in my back so that when I dropped it my arms went all tingly and numb. I could not move my arms at all for several minutes. Did I go to sick call? Nope.

# CHAPTER 3: BECOMING AN NCO

**EVENTUALLY MY HAZING STOPPED WHEN** new soldiers came in that really were soup sandwiches. Sometime between 2004 and 2005, I went to Primary leadership development course (PLDC) and was pinned sergeant shortly afterward. Then I was formally welcomed to the club. Here's where the military gets quite quirky. I basically went from zero to hero overnight. I was being hazed one day and then I built up my promotional points, became an E4 promotable specialist, went to the board, and they sent me to PLDC. Now I was an E5 sergeant and I was immediately put into the next leadership role. I became Alpha team leader, which is one step down from the squad leader and a step above Bravo team leader. And here's where I found out how David Wellington's saying came into being: *shit rolls downhill; bureaucracy rolls faster.* We would have company formations the first thing in the morning where the orders for the day would come from the first sergeant and the commanding officer (CO). After the formation was done, platoon sergeants and leaders would reiterate the orders and pass them down to the squad leaders. After that formation, the squad leaders would have their squad formations and break down the orders to the team leaders, mostly Alpha team leader. After that formation, team leaders executed the orders with the three to five soldiers they had in their command. If we did a good job, everyone above got praised. If we did a bad job, it all rolled downhill and landed in the team leader's lap.

The learning curve jumped really fast. One day I was taking orders and the next day I was giving them. As the old Spiderman saying goes, *with great power comes great responsibility.* Every now and then I had the opportunity to lead PT. When running, I was expected to join in leading the call-and-response work songs we call cadences. I even started going to training courses with my platoon sergeant. He jokingly yet also seriously told me he was going to take a nap while I learned the training and then I would teach it to everybody else, while he nodded his head; you know, one of those *train the trainer* things. I also had to council my Alpha team every month in attempt to help them further their own military careers. Truly, this was great training! This is the type of leadership I was built for. Leading soldiers was one of my favorite things to do!

# CHAPTER 4: REFORMATION AND RECRUITS

**NOW I WAS A SERGEANT,** part of the *backbone of the Army.* Early 2005 rolled around and we got a new batch of recruits. We also got a new batch of NCOs, a new first sergeant, a new company commander, and new *butter bars*, which was what we called second lieutenants. There were lots of moving pieces at this time. This is when the Army went through a large restructuring. Instead of being separated by military occupational specialty (MOS), we were grouped with and attached to several other support specialties in a new battalion that was directly attached to an infantry brigade. Our old combat engineer battalion was disbanded, and Charlie Company Zone was no more. We were renamed Alpha Company, Third Brigade, Special Troops Battalion (A3STB).

With all the new soldiers and officers, our whole company was restructured as well. A few new people that came to us were company commander Captain Corsetti, First Sergeant Harmand, First Lieutenant Shaw, Platoon Sergeant First Class Savage, Sergeant Willard, and Second Squad leader Staff Sergeant Fowler. There were many others, but this group was basically my chain of command. A few soldiers I will mention later that came to our squad were Specialists Weiss and Merrick and Privates Doyle, Owens, and Pauley.

Here is some information on a few people in our company that should give you some insight into the overall outcome and story of this book. First, Captain Corsetti: he was an NCO that later became an officer, which is called going from *green to gold*. He used to be an instructor at Sapper School, and was a graduate of Ranger School, both intensely rigorous training programs that most people couldn't complete. With my limited knowledge of military lingo at the time, I thought he was all *tabbed out*. You know that song by Jim Croce, "You Don't Mess Around with Jim?" Yeah, I think they wrote that about him. He was very strict, but fair. He expected nothing but the best, period. His goal was to make us not only the best we could be, but the best unit in the brigade entirely. All the training we did was grueling, but he had so many connections that about anything he asked for, he got. He had a double-crooked nose, as if it had been broken more than once, and had this look on his face as if to say, "go ahead, just try to mess with me." Believe me there was no way that anybody wanted to mess with him.

Next, First Sergeant Harmand: he was an injured paratrooper that used to be part of an elite team of paratroopers that jumped into stadiums and other places for special events. He walked and ran with a very noticeable limp, but you would not hear him complain about it.

Third, Platoon Sergeant First Class Savage: early in his career he reclassified from being a cook to being a combat engineer but you would've never known it. He was this five-foot, four-inch PT powerhouse. He could've been a drill sergeant. He was mostly soft spoken, but there was no way you wanted to make him mad.

Next, squad leader Staff Sergeant Fowler: he had just come from a mechanized unit in Germany and our squad was his first squad to lead. He was kind of wishy-washy. He would horseplay around and then quick as that turn around and be serious and start screaming at his soldiers, a bit like Dr. Jekyll and Mr. Hyde. You just didn't know which one you were going to get on any given day.

We also got Sergeant Willard, who became Bravo team leader and, in my opinion, should have become Alpha team leader. He easily had at least ten years of service on me and I was barely in my second year of service. This guy knew his stuff, was tough on privates, loved to banter with anyone, and he was super hilarious. He was the guy you wanted around just to get your mind to forget crap. He always made me laugh.

Then there was Specialist Merrick, who also just came from Germany, who had a wealth of combat engineer knowledge. He was very smart, but also very immature at the time.

We also got Specialist Weiss, who had a lot of soldiering knowledge, outdoorsman knowledge, and in my opinion, should have been in my position as team leader instead of me. I felt inferior to him, but his respect for me was amazing. I would even say that he was a soldier's soldier. I respected him a lot.

Private Doyle also joined us. Wow. That guy was truly a soup sandwich. He had many nicknames. We called him *The General's Daughter* because he was literally the son of a general, so we made fun of him by referring to him as a daughter. I was told by some of his fellow basic trainees that he should not have made it through basic training, but his father was able to pull strings so he could make it. He was also named *Can'tgetright* because he just couldn't. He was a PT stud, but he had no common sense. Finally, he was called *Spiderman* because he fell from the second-floor barracks window, breaking both of his lower legs while trying to rappel from the third floor to open his window on the second floor. Someone had played a prank on him and locked him out of his room. He was in Air Assault School at the time and had a thirteen-and-a-half-foot rope that he was supposed to be practicing tying his Swiss-seat harness with. That rope is what he rappelled with, while two other *Joes* held the other end of the rope from the third floor. Needless to say, he did not get into his room and either the belt loop that he was repelling from broke or the other guys simply just dropped him. He fell and broke both his legs right in front of the pizza delivery guy. You can't make this stuff up! This happened about a month before we deployed to Iraq. He should have never gone with us! But alas, the *General's Daughter* struck again.

And then there was Private Owens or *Pretty Boy*, as we called him. He was one of those guys that was too cool for school. He was sly, slick, and smart, and not too shabby with the ladies either, or at least he said so. He also became our squad's marksman.

The last soldier I want to mention is Private Anthony Pauley. I remember the day that these soldiers came to the unit, especially Pvt. Pauley. He was scrawny, pimply faced, wore glasses, walked awkwardly, and was just goofy in general. He usually had a crooked smile on his face, and he was super pumped that he was a soldier altogether because it was in his blood. Pauley's father used to be a combat medic and he had two older brothers in the military at that time, *two in the box* for the two Army brothers, and *one in the pond* for the Navy brother, as Anthony used to say. He was very proud to be there to carry on the legacy of his family. But because of Pauley's characteristics mentioned before, he often got picked on and was hazed regularly by some of the other soldiers. He was an easy target. He was my soldier, and I was his direct supervisor. I never hazed him. In my life I have always been drawn to the underdog and they to me. It's just one of the things that I have always done; I stick up for the guy who can't stick up for himself. I thought Pauley's hazing would stop on its own, but it did not, so I had to get involved and tell the guys to stop doing it. Needless to say, Pauley became quite attached to me since I looked out for him. But the hazing had already done its work and Pauley had lost confidence in his abilities. From the way things stood I did not think it was safe for Pauley to stay with us, so I began to look for ways for him to reclassify. But as we will find out later, not only did that not happen, but it was also thwarted from happening for him.

# CHAPTER 5: GOING TO WAR

**WE GOT ORDERS TO GO** to Iraq in early 2005 right around the same time as all of the changes I mentioned were taking place. This foreshadowed the coming of a very tough year. We began training on just about every aspect you could think of. We trained in hand-to-hand combat, advanced medical training, including giving someone an IV. We trained and qualified on every weapon type we could: M4/M16 rifle, M203 grenade launcher, M249 machine gun, shotgun, 240B machine gun, .50-caliber machine gun, AT4 rocket launcher, and Mk 19 machine grenade launcher. I also trained on the Javelin anti-tank missile, but we were never given one. Two other weapons a few trained on were the M9 pistol and the M14 sniper rifle. Our division was an air assault division, so everyone that did not have that badge yet was rushed through Air Assault School. We went to the firing range as much as we could for day and night training. We acquired EOTECH holographic weapon sights with red dot scopes for our M4s and a few green-beam lasers—real science fiction stuff. We also began to do PT twice a day. We did paintball military operations on urban terrain (MOUT) training and a little shoot house training. To meet Army Corps of Engineers requirements we had to complete a twenty-mile ruck march with very specific standards (a total suck fest) and go to the demo range to arm and disarm a live mine in addition to our typical practice with C4 explosives and Detonation (DET) cord. There were other requirements we had to fulfill before we went to Iraq, but I truly can't remember everything.

During this time Platoon Sfc. Savage asked us if there would be any important dates that would happen during our deployment, like getting married or having a baby or something like that. I told him that my first child was scheduled to be born in early March. He asked for the date and I gave it to him. This was so we could plan a schedule for rest and relaxation (R&R) leave, which we were all entitled to during our one-year deployment. He told me I could either have two weeks before the date or two weeks after the date, so I chose two weeks after the date just in case the pregnancy was late.

We were leaving for Iraq in September, but sometime in June a decision was made to go to Fort Knox for additional MOUT training, shoot house training, and a new advanced firing range training called close quarters combat (CQC). One blistering night that June we left at zero-dark-thirty, air-assaulting by helicopter into Ft. Knox from Fort Campbell. It would have been really awesome if I wasn't really fed up with all the training already. We did a few days of advanced MOUT training in a mock middle eastern village against opposing force (OPFOR) soldiers with live sim-paint rounds. Those little stinking rounds could actually break the skin and gave quite a sting and a lasting welt. During the MOUT training, this mock village kept setting off flash and smoke grenades, and there was really loud Middle Eastern music. They had a mosque that played propaganda on a recorded loudspeaker constantly. It was information overload. I believe they also had live tracer rounds shooting over our heads during the training where we could see the trajectory of the bullets.

It was cool but intense. Part of our training was also sleeping in this village at night with twenty-four-hour guard posts. One night after this training, a group of my soldiers were staying on a second-floorarea and needed to peein the middle of the night. Instead of going down to a port-a-potty, they decided to pee off of the balcony. It just so happened that at the same time the second platoon sergeant was smoking a cigarette or something on the first floor underneath that balcony, and he got pissed on. In the morning, after a good night's rest, the news that the second platoon sergeant was pissed on got to our platoon sergeant and he was raging. It was discovered that my soldier, Pauley, had peed off of the balcony in the night onto the second platoon sergeant. I was instructed to *smoke* the daylights out of Pauley, so I had him get his 240B machine gun and I took him outside. I had him do lunges around our Humvee with his machine gun over his head. He didn't last long, maybe not even two minutes, and he began to actually cry. My platoon sergeant could hear it from the building, and he commanded me to stop. I was glad because I hated doing that type of stuff, but I knew it was necessary.

Next, we did a few days of dry fire shoot-house training over and over and over and over and over and over again. I can't tell you how many different scenarios of shoot-house training we did. It was good but grueling. All of that to build up to a day of live fire shoot-house training. The shoot house is a kind of indoor firing range that is set up to look like a possible home of an enemy so we can practice clearing rooms or breaching doors, like we might do in an urban combat situation. During the live fire training we only had to clear one room and it was to get us used to firing in close-quarters-combat with one another. To make it more real, the enemy silhouettes that were in the room for us to shoot had ketchup packets placed on them. As Alpha team leader I was the number one man, so I had to go the farthest in the room and have the opportunity for the most people to shoot targets that were only about ten feet from my final

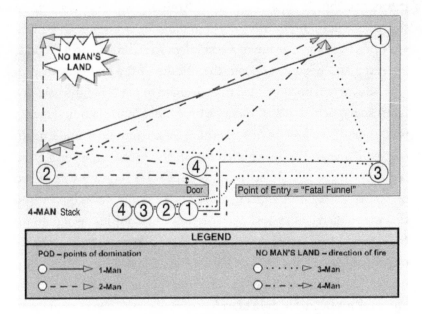

*Shoot house training diagram.*

position. I'm glad Pvt. Owens was the number two man, because he was our squad marksman. This was another intense training.

Finally, we did many days of endless range time with advance close-quarter-combat training. We fired so many rounds our rifle muzzles began to have a reddish glow. I was thanking God when we ran out of bullets, but then somehow the CO got 60,000 more, and when we ran out of them, he called in a favor and got 30,000 more. We just kept getting more and more rounds. I have no idea how many we actually shot. So, here's the scenario: one whole platoon would stand on the firing line just about shoulder to shoulder firing all at the same time, and we would left face and turn at the hip and fire all at the same time. Then we would right face and do the same thing, and then we would strife and do the same thing, move forward and shoot in unison and backward, too. We would take a knee together, lie prone together, and shoot all the same time. This is close-quarter combat. Being so close together with all the ejection ports on the right side of our rifles, sometimes the ejected hot casing would go into the shirt of the guy to the right, causing an intense neck or back burn from the casing. It was like being branded like a cow. Suddenly someone on the line would jump up and down, screaming in pain and shock. But after it happened once, and because the first sergeant and the CO wanted you to grin and bear it, you would grit your teeth and stay online and continue to fire with everyone else not missing a beat. I'm pretty sure we all got a few of these burns. I know I did.

This brings me to another important part of this story. Remember Pauley? We were on the firing line shooting and shooting endlessly, or so it seemed. We were about to start our next iteration and I was going up and down the line making sure everyone in my charge was ready. The next thing I knew, Pvt. Owens got my attention and had a serious look on his face when he told me that he overheard Pvt. Pauley saying that he was thinking of killing himself during this iteration. I told my squad leader, S.Sgt. Fowler, and he immediately went straight to Pauley and told him to go ahead and kill himself while screaming and yelling profanities at him (in typical Army fashion). Luckily, others in command overheard all of this. I was instructed to take his weapon from him, take him off the line, bring him back to our tent, and to relax and cool down. Pauley was in a bad place. When we got back to the tent after turning our weapons in to our armory, I began to counsel Pauley and get him thinking positive thoughts about his family and possibly about getting out of our unit, which I really think was the best thing for him. I thought maybe this would be the catalyst to get orders for him to go somewhere else. I believed he just did not belong with us and he would fare better in a different job. Pauley was a good guy, but he was not cut from the same cloth as the other roughnecks. After an hour or so, I was relieved by another NCO and instructed to go and speak with the first sergeant. So, I went to see 1st Sgt. Harmand and in not so many words he said Pauley was not going anywhere. In fact, no one was, because everyone was going to Iraq. Next, the first sergeant told me that I could no longer protect Pauley, and instead of being his advocate, I would start to have to be hard on him. No more special treatment for Pauley. This was not what I expected to hear and a knot in my stomach grew. I hated what I was being commanded to do. After this conversation, I went back to Pauley and relayed the message to him and advised him on how I would be treating him from then on. To Pauley's credit, he received this news respectfully and without question.

After Fort Knox, and for the next few weeks of additional training as mentioned above, I began to see a transformation in Pauley. Somehow, he grew in confidence and his mood changed from downtrodden to happy-go-lucky. I couldn't believe the change that took place before my eyes. I could tell Pauley to go choke out the biggest guy in our unit and he would try to do it. Of course, he would fail and get choked out himself instead, but he was confident the whole time. He was a new man, and I was very proud of him. He was turning twenty-one and he was making plans to get married after Iraq. He was asking for relationship advice from my wife and I. I didn't know it at the time, but I began to love this kid like he was my son.

We were leaving for Iraq in September. Our command was desperately trying to jam-pack every type of training we could still get in. The opportunity for me to go for a month-long training came up called Sapper School. Was I ready for this? Hell no, but they sent me anyway. My mind was not prepared for this training although it was going to be an elite training. I'm not sure if this was July or August, but we drove to Fort Leonard Wood and we got situated for a day or so before the training began. I was all nerves, and the night before it began, I drank way too much water. About four o'clock in the morning I woke up and had to piss like a racehorse and I should have immediately hydrated but I did not. I'm not sure I slept much that night anyway, but they came and got us before the sun came up to start our PT test to begin the school. I had a dry mouth and I knew I was not going to do well. I just so happened to be the first one in line, yay! Normally I could max out the score on sit-ups and push-ups. But I was extremely dehydrated, and during the first event of push-ups I don't even think I got to fifty before I started to see stars and blacked out. The next thing I knew, I woke up with an IV in my arm, on a gurney, being pushed down the hall in the hospital. That meant an immediate no-go for me, and I was not allowed back into the Sapper School training. I was disappointed and relieved at the same time and they said that I would have to stay there doing busy work while everyone else went through the training. I explained to the commandant that we were going to Iraq within the next month, and I would like to go back home and spend that time with my wife. He understood, but he left it up to my company commander. I called my CO and explained to him what had happened, and he graciously allowed me to return home. I hitched a ride with some soldiers that had just completed the school and were going back to Fort Campbell (thanks guys, you were awesome!).

When I got back to the unit, it was all the same stuff—constant training. It was pretty much a blur and shortly after the other guys got back from Sapper School, it was down to days or weeks from us leaving to go to Iraq. Then the day for us to leave came and all of our families were invited to see us off. That is when my beautiful bride begged to go with me. She wanted to be packed secretly away in my stuff so that we would not be separated. Through many tears and embraces the time finally came for us to go. We gathered our gear and were bussed to the on-base airport tarmac, where we waited to board our commercial flight to Kuwait.

# CHAPTER 6: THE WAIT IN KUWAIT

**WHEN WE ALL GOT ON** that commercial flight at Fort Campbell, it felt like going to Basic Training all over again. Going into the unknown. The first flight was to someplace on the East Coast, where we had a short break. Then we flew to Germany, where we had a few hours of layover. And then we were back on the plane again to fly to Kuwait in the middle of the night. I'm not sure when it happened, but on one of those flights I remember sitting there in my seat surrounded by everyone else in their military uniforms and all holding our personal weapons in our laps. It hit me: we're going to war. The thought occurred to me for the very first time that I may die, or I may have to kill someone. I was immediately gripped by fear and a deep, overwhelming dread. And just as fast, I closed my eyes and silently prayed and gave my fears to God. From that moment on I had a peace about those two things. I was mentally prepared for whatever came next.

When we left from Germany to fly into Kuwait at night, I

remember vividly knowing instinctively at one point that we were flying over Iraq. As I looked out the window, I saw almost nothing, barely any lights to know that there was life down below us. But then, in the distance there was one bright light, and as we drew closer it began to take shape. Getting even closer it became the unmistakable shape of the country of Kuwait, just like an image from a physical map. And in stark contrast to its surroundings, the country of Kuwait was lit up like a Christmas tree, like a beacon, like a lighthouse guiding our plane. It was truly an inspiring site.

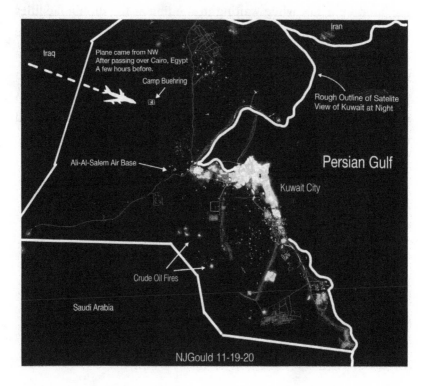

*Drawing of satellite image. Original artwork by Nathan Gould.*

This part of the journey was very boring and redundant, as our unit became lost in the sea of other units waiting for orders. It was a logistical nightmare. We felt like we were minuscule bricks in a huge box of Legos, waiting for someone to choose us. But the creators were only searching for just the right piece to use for the project they were building, and they could not find it either. It probably was only three or four weeks, but it felt like months just sitting in Kuwait. But we didn't just sit there, we somehow found more training to do. It just felt like there was a job that we were supposed to do, and we want to get it done. I often thought to myself, *Can we just start already and get this over with so we can go home?* It was a very frustrating time.

There was another seemingly insignificant event that happened there that I must share because it would become important to me later. One day, while waiting in the line at the dining facilities administration center (DFAC), some random corporal—who must've just gotten his rank—walked up from behind me and began to ream out Weiss for something that was wrong with his uniform. He even made Weiss start doing push-ups. I was glaring at the corporal, who was trying to chum up to me. He had just disrespected my man and me in front of hundreds of people. I still kick myself for not smoking him right there. Weiss had a good attitude though, he laughed it off and chuckled to himself, but I was upset that it had happened. The rest of our time in Kuwait was much of the same. We just trained and trained and trained until we got orders to go somewhere else.

# CHAPTER 7: FOB SUMMERALL

**WHEN WE FINALLY GOT ORDERS** to go somewhere else, it was first to another training base, but I don't really remember too much about that one. It was really just more training and waiting around. Although I do remember qualifying on my M203 grenade launcher and the .50-caliber machine gun there. Actually, I think it was while we were there that I got my nickname of *Father* because I was spiritual and prayed. Then after another few weeks we were ordered to go to Forward Operating Base Summerall.

At this point, we still did not have specific orders for where we would serve during our stay in Iraq; we were still waiting for those. But in the meantime, we got our vehicles ready and assigned to us. Then we were given a temporary living area, which was basically an empty warehouse with makeshift partition walls so we all could have separate sleeping areas. Soon we were given the task of route clearance and security. We were tasked with the time from dusk until dawn for this activity. Every night we would leave at dusk and patrol the surrounding area and Route 1 to ensure improvised explosive device (IED) suppression and prevention. My first taste of death came on one of those evenings that we had set up a roadblock to check vehicles for IEDs randomly. It must've been early morning, because there was a mandatory curfew for all of Iraq from dusk until dawn. No vehicles were supposed to be on the roads, not to mention that all Iraqi nationals were supposed to be in their homes as well. We had checked vehicles for a few hours and then just held traffic. I don't remember what for specifically, but we did it. We sat there in the middle of the road with about a quarter mile between two trucks on one side holding up traffic and two trucks on the other end of the quarter mile holding up traffic. Also, our command truck was somewhere at a high spot in the middle watching over all of us. As we were just sitting there in the quiet of night, machine gun fire shattered the silence. I remember turning to see the other two trucks on the opposite end of our blockade lighting up this vehicle with machine gun fire and then the vehicle bursting into flames. The violence of this action was so quick and precise I could feel the heat of the vehicle that was immediately engulfed in flames. It's so odd looking back at this, I don't even remember talking to the guys who fired their weapons that night and took another person's life. It wouldn't be the last time, either, and it always seemed there was nothing to say. How do you talk about it?

Our schedule at Summerall was quite nice, come to think of it. We went on missions every other day, switching out with Second Platoon. On the nights we didn't go on a mission we had some downtime and could actually do some type of recreation-like weightlifting or playing basketball, but that didn't last long.

As we went on our bi-nightly missions we began mapping the area for ourselves. In doing this we found that there was what appeared to be an oil refinery nearby that had a high fence with guard towers all the way around it. Naturally we decided to check it out. We embarked on a dismounted patrol on the road surrounding the refinery. It was a quiet, cold night and our dismounted patrol was marching in a V

formation. Merrick and I were walking in the sand between the fence
of the refinery and the road when suddenly a shot rang out. Because of
the silence, the echo could be heard very well. I heard a whizzing noise
zip through the silence, which meant the shot was a near miss. Merrick
and I hit the deck hard. We could not see where the shot came from,
but we both fixed our sights on the guard tower about two hundred
yards to our left front. We would have used our night vision goggles
(NVG), but there were bright spotlights on every guard tower and on
the top of the fences facing the ground. I had a handheld radio at that
time and asked if we should return fire on the guard tower. They took
a minute to respond, since they all were probably attempting to find
cover in the barren wasteland. I don't remember the specific answer
I got back, but it was along the lines that I should decide for myself.
Merrick and I did not shoot, and there were no other shots. After a
while, our interpreter came and spoke with whoever was in the guard
tower and we confiscated that guard's Russian-made rifle and then we
took over his guard post for the rest of the night too. The guard stayed
with us in the tower and fell asleep while we stayed awake, freezing.
The next morning, we entered the oil refinery and took a good look
around and found a huge cache of anti-aircraft artillery (AAA) rounds.
We loaded up all of our vehicles with as much as we could carry and
brought them back to the FOB. We went back until that whole pile was
gone. Then, with a sense of accomplishment, we walked a little farther
up over a hill and found many other huge piles of these AAA rounds.
After some investigation, we discovered that these AAA rounds were
all inert and useless since they had been sitting there from the first
Gulf War about ten years earlier. We left the rest of the piles where
they lay and did not go back.

Sometime during one of these missions, one of our drivers, Pvt.
Doyle, was burning the candle on both ends and decided he could stay
up during the day and at night if he just drank enough Wild Tiger energy
drinks. On patrol one night, the Second Squad truck was bringing up
the rear of the convoy while traveling using the red black-out lights

and our NVGs. Second Squad just stopped, and the rest of the convoy kept going for a few miles until they realized Second Squad was not there. The convoy had to turn around and go find Second Squad, who happened to all be fast asleep in their truck. Sgt. Fowler got reamed out, as did Pvt. Doyle, who was the driver. That is when Pvt. Doyle was fired from being the driver and replaced with Spc. Weiss.

The next thing of extreme significance that occurred was during one of our days off. Pvt. Pauley approached me and explained that he was not feeling very confident in his ability as a soldier to do what might need to be done when a time for action or violence may come. As we had been in different trucks during missions, we did not get to spend much time together anymore. I could tell he was struggling with his confidence, so I took him to the warehouse right next to ours that was empty, and we practiced wrestling in hand-to-hand combat for a while. Then we walked to the middle of the warehouse and I told him that I was going to walk to the front door of the building, and if he allowed me to leave the warehouse, he would have hell to pay. I told him I would smoke the crap out of him. I told him he would not get in trouble and to do whatever he needed to do to stop me from leaving. Then I started walking, and I'm happy to say, I did not make it out of the warehouse. Pauley accomplished the mission. He regained his confidence.

Then came a day I will never forget. First Platoon was on a mission that night and it had been uneventful until we were on our way back to base, just before sunup. We were patrolling down Route 1 toward an overpass when we saw two Iraqi national (IN) young men standing on the side of the road next to a white pickup truck with their hands raised in the air, as if to surrender. Initially our convoy drove right past them and we were going to ignore them and go back to base, like we had planned. I was looking forward to getting some sleep. But Lt. Shaw and Platoon Sgt. Savage decided to turn around and check them out. We quickly turned around, immediately setting up a security night assistance patrol traffic control point (SNAP TCP). Two trucks went forward, two trucks stayed back, one went up on the hill, and our third squad truck drove up fast and dismounted to check out these guys. Merrick and I were told to frisk the Iraqi young men and so we began to walk toward them. As we did S.Sgt. Bell yelled out that there were AAA rounds all over the ground in the area with wires coming out of them. S.Sgt. Pearson yelled at us to get right back in the truck, so Merrick and I ran back to the truck and hopped in. The driver slammed down the gas in reverse and we sped backwards, off the road and out of the danger zone, because some of the wired-up ordinance had been underneath our vehicle. Then Merrick and I dismounted, charging toward the Iraqis again. We subdued them and put them in zip cuffs. We searched them and found nothing. We searched the vehicle and found nothing. Then we set them on the side the road. After closer inspection of the AAA rounds that had wires attached to them, we found they were inert. They would not have exploded because there wasn't any detonation device attached to them yet. We put in a call to the explosive ordinance disposal (EOD) team for disposal. We were instructed that EOD would come when they were ready, and we needed to wait. So we sat there waiting for EOD. While we waited, curfew was lifted, and the Iraqi people began to go about their daily business. Imagine a flat desert landscape almost all the way around us. The road that we were on was pretty straight north and south and the cars started to pile up on both sides of us as far as we could see on that two-lane road. Over time this became more like ten to twenty lanes across on each side and the longer we held traffic, the more vehicles arrived. Then everybody toward the front of the traffic jam, probably ten to twenty vehicles back, got out and walked up to the source of the traffic jam. They became a mob speaking in languages we could not understand. This was a recipe for disaster. People were milling all around. Some were praying to the east on their little prayer mats. Others were sitting around eating. It would've been a perfect time to put a roadside bomb somewhere in the midst of all that confusion, and I truly believe that is when those things happen. The sun had only begun to rise somewhere beneath the horizon when we began to hear very clearly what sounded like machine gun fire nearby. Everyone heard it and began to take cover. No one said anything at first, as if we were in shock, but then Spc. Gilchrist, who was in the turret of the Third Squad truck that day, broke the silence and asked me if I heard the gunfire. I agreed that I did hear it and I reluctantly relayed this information over my handheld radio. Then the message was passed on to higher command. Suddenly our situation became important enough to do something about. The quick reaction force (QRF) was called for us, but they were sleeping. Capt. Corsetti was pissed off, to say the least. He and 1st Sgt. Harmand had been awake with us during this whole time and Second Platoon had already geared up waiting for orders to go and help us. Capt. Corsetti basically said to screw QRF, that they were going to go help their own guys! So they mounted up, including Second Squad from First Platoon, who had the day off, and headed our way. As they approached our position, an unknown vehicle entered the middle of their convoy and Capt. Corsetti told whoever was closest to it to deal with it. It just so happened that it was the Second Squad vehicle from First Platoon that was closest to the unknown vehicle. The decision was made to ram it instead of shooting at it. So they rammed the pick-up truck

*Moment of impact 2nd squad rammed the Iraqi vehicle that entered the convoy.*
*Original artwork by Nathan J. Gould.*

and as they did reports from Second Platoon said that they saw a large flash and then the Second Squad vehicle began to roll. The doors flew off and the contents of the vehicle were thrown about and out, including all of the passengers. In the meantime, back at our position we kept hearing the machine gun fire close by us, but we could not see where the bullets were coming from or where they were going. Within a few minutes, two Apache helicopters showed up and began to circle our area looking for the source of the gunfire. The Apache pilots asked us where we thought it was coming from. We told them we did not know, and they began to circle in ever increasing larger circles. The gunfire was cyclical, and you could probably time the sound of it to about every thirty seconds. We started to get antsy because Second Platoon was not showing up yet, but unbeknownst to us, or at least everyone who was dismounted and did not have a radio, Second Platoon had also been attacked. Within the next few minutes a few things happened. The sun came up enough for us to see our surroundings pretty good and that's when we discovered the source of the machine gun fire. My heart dropped when I saw it because it was not a machine gun at all. It was what appeared to be farming equipment, which was probably an irrigation system or pump of some sort. It appeared to run on diesel fuel and had a smokestack with a spring-loaded metallic flap that made a distinct sound and spewed smoke every thirty seconds. It sounded just like a machine gun. I could have thrown up right there, I was so sick to my stomach when I saw that. I really think everyone felt the same way, but I blamed myself for making the report of it. Also, in those few minutes a cavalry scout (CAV) unit replaced us to wait for EOD so we could go help Second Platoon. We loaded up our two prisoners and drove to where Second Platoon was holding up traffic, about two miles from our location. The only people that knew what had happened in First Platoon were the drivers and whoever else had a radio. They were told specifically not to tell anyone else so all could keep their heads in the game. I was one of the people who did not know what had happened to Second Platoon. When we drove to them stopped in the roadway, we saw medevac helicopters flying away and wrecker vehicles picking up a destroyed Humvee and a shot-up pick-up truck. It was very confusing. I remember a white sheet draped over a body on a gurney being loaded into a medevac. As soon as we got to the scene, we were told to dismount again and pull security. I tried to gain contact with someone from Second Platoon, but they would not give me any eye contact. Almost as soon as we got there, Second Platoon left and went back to base. We stood there pulling security until the wrecker trucks were ready to leave. As one of the wreckers drove by Merrick got a glance at the call sign on the back bumper of the Humvee and it was the call sign for First Platoon, Second Squad which was our squad, our guys. Before we left with the wrecker trucks, one of the oddest things I've ever seen happened. A unit showed up to replace us, but they were not American, they were Iraqi. The best way I can explain them is they appeared to be like Iraqi Special Forces. They had way cooler digital American-made uniforms, but they did not have helmets on, and they even had spiked and gelled hair. One of them had a gold-plated AK-47 and they immediately took the scene away from us and began to corral the Iraqi people. I was so tired at this point I couldn't even form the words to say thank you before we left. We returned to base sometime close to noon, dropped everybody off at the warehouse and then Merrick and I continued on to turn in our prisoners to the holding cells for interrogation. Then we returned back to our warehouse to finally unload our personal gear and hopefully get rest. As soon as we drove up S.Sgt. Pearson met us at our Humvee with tears streaming down his face and told us what had happened to Second Squad's vehicle. He said that when they had rammed the pick-up truck the Humvee went into an unrecoverable roll and the doors flew off. The gunner, Pauley, had slammed his head into the butt of the mounted 240B machine gun upon impact. Weiss, who I was told was the driver that day, had his chest crushed by the unsecured radio from the radio mount. S.Sgt. Fowler had a broken femur, Sgt. Willard had a few broken ribs and a broken upper arm and Pvt. Doyle had a broken back. In short, the whole squad was wiped out. Everyone was on the way to an Army hospital in Germany and no one would be coming back. He said that Weiss was dead and that Pauley had been pronounced brain dead. Upon hearing this news Merrick sat on the ground and cried. I stood there in shock. I walked into our warehouse and everyone seemed to be avoiding everyone else. You could hear stifled sniffles everywhere. Before I had a chance to put down my stuff, I was approached by Sgt. Yarwood who, without batting an eye, asked me to sign a release on Weiss' and Pauley's personal gear so it could be sent to their families. I was so emotionally spent that, even though I was not sure if this was proper procedure, I began to attempt to fill out the paperwork just to get him out of my face. That's when the first sergeant overheard what was happening and stopped Yarwood before I signed anything. For goodness sake, some of Weiss's bloody gear was at my feet at that very moment, what the hell was he thinking? Then I finally went to my bunk and laid down and I don't remember much else until an evening formation was called. In this formation it was confirmed that Weiss was dead. Pauley was still brain dead, and now his parents had decided to pull the plug. At hearing that news I became red hot with anger. I was not ready for Pauley to be dead. He was like a son to me. I was truly seeing red. After the formation I knew we had gained a new truck and that it had to be fitted with our gear. I asked to go down to the garage to work on the truck because I needed something to distract me. They told me I could go, and they sent all the Joes with me. This work was actually somewhat therapeutic for me and probably for the other Joes too.

During this very difficult time, I received a very untimely letter from my mother. The letter's message accused me of being a warmonger and a mercenary of sorts. But then her words struck a nerve by ignorantly saying that I joined the workings of the devil when I joined the Army, and I would be a terrible father and abusive husband just like my father. I wrote her back, saying that she had no idea what I was going through and that if I or my wife ever received another letter like that, or my wife and unborn child heard any wind of that kind of talk, I would disown her and she would never meet her grandchildren. Those types of letters never came again. She really pissed me off, especially after my comrades had just died. I will never understand what possessed her to send that hate-mail to her own son.

Sometime that week the company had a memorial service at FOB Summerall for Weiss and Pauley. Each of us marched up to an empty pair of boots that had a rifle propped up from inside one of them and a Kevlar helmet perched on top of the muzzle, symbolizing a fallen comrade. We saluted toward this gear to honor their memory, then marched away again. This ceremony only fed my anger and hate for war in general. I did not realize it, but I began to be hypervigilant, in a constant state of increased alertness and sensitivity to my surroundings, and whatever optimism and spiritualism I had before that, just stopped. We got to Iraq in early September and this incident happened on November 17; we had a long year ahead of us.

# CHAPTER 8: DRINK WATER, DRIVE ON MENTALITY

**AFTER LOSING SECOND SQUAD THINGS** changed. Another unit took over our nightly route patrols, but we still went out on patrols and did stationary route overwatch until we were finally assigned our own company mission. We were to take over possession of Patrol Base Razor from the 82nd Airborne Division, which was formally used as an Iraqi police (IP) station. PB Razor was located on the Tigris River, adjacent to a hydroelectric dam that provided electricity for Northern Iraq and Baghdad. The plant was between two bridges. One bridge led north into the larger city of Samarra where the Golden Mosque, one of the four major Shi'ite shrines in Iraq, still stood. The other bridge led south to the small town of Hueish. PB Razor was literally on the edge of another small village directly east of us called Qulah. We spent about a week with the 82nd Airborne, seeing how they ran things and slowly taking over from them. After they left, our command decided to beef up the base. Mostly, we filled sandbags and fortified the defenses that were already there and placed them on top of our living quarters for defense against the mortar and rocket attacks that came almost nightly.

That reminds me of the war that we were fighting. It was strictly guerrilla tactics. All the bad guys look just like the good guys. You couldn't tell who was good and who was bad. It's not like they were an established military force with uniforms and insignia that pointed them out, like there were saying *hey, here I am*, like the coalition forces. Yeah, we got to run around with targets on our backs because of our uniforms and all of the obvious signs that we were US soldiers and coalition forces, but they got to wear their man-dresses and walk around in our midst and we didn't even know it. They were just individuals acting out, or insurgents, as the American media liked to call them. These extremists were not as extreme as you would think. They didn't want to die. So what did they do? They mostly attacked at night. They put their IEDs in under the cover of darkness, they carried out mortar attacks and shot rockets almost blindly at night and then they ran. They would only shoot two or three rockets or mortars and then they would run like chickens. If they got somebody, great! If they didn't, they waited a few days and shot some more. The Islamic State of Iraq and Syria (ISIS), in my opinion, was a bunch of cowards. They even kidnapped their own people, strapped bombs to them and sent them to kill coalition forces because if the IED with a brain didn't do it, their whole family would die at the hands of ISIS. Where is the honor in that? That's my soapbox on that issue.

Our new mission at PB Razor became: number one, don't let the hydroelectric dam get blown up. Number two, prevent IEDs from being placed on our section of the Huiesh cut and Route 1. Number three, don't let the bridges get blown up. The 82nd Airborne already had two guard posts outside of the base that we took over, but we added another one at the end of the Huiesh cut, where it intersected with Route 1. All these guard posts would end up being manned continuously around the clock. At PB Razor we were the only company there running the base, so we had to get a few attachments of other support units to help us out with things we were lacking, like communication, medical personnel, and a mortar squad. Also, during this time we were given new engineer soldiers to replace the ones that had been lost to rebuild Second Squad. Eventually everything became routine. Every other week First Platoon and Second Platoon would switch missions. One week would be guard duty most of the day and night and also go to farther places like FOB Brassfield-Mora to get needed supplies. Then the following week our platoons would switch missions.

During one of the weeks where First Platoon had guard duty on base, I got a tailbone injury while I was on roving guard duty checking on the guys at different guard posts. I was walking down a makeshift ladder and sat down quick because I had lost my balance and I slammed straight down onto a piece of rebar. The pain from this injury didn't go away for several days and I had to stand up as straight as I could and sit as straight as I could, and it was hard to sleep. I finally went to see the medical doctor about it several days later, but they couldn't do too much for me except to document the incident.

Also during one of these weeks of guard duty, I was on one of the mounted .50-cal. machine guns that overlooked the snake-shaped serpentine barrier into our base. I had just relieved another soldier at

*Me on the .50-cal. guarding the serpentine entrance to PB Razor.*

guard. After changing guard, we are supposed to unload and reload the weapon at that location as procedure. I unloaded and reloaded the .50-cal. machine gun and then I pressed the trigger, as this was part of the clearing procedure at the time. One single shot rang out and scared me half to death. At that very moment I looked up and saw a small whisk of dust floating off the ground near a Jersey barrier used to separate lines of traffic, about 1000 yards in front of me, which was about two feet away from an Iraqi Army (IA) soldier directing traffic in the street, who dove behind the Jersey barrier. My heart was beating a million beats a minute because ten degrees to my left was a guard post and ten degrees to my right was another guard post. The .50-cal. round, *thank God*, threaded that needle and also missed the soldier in the street. Everyone heard it, and I expected to be replaced at guard, but no, radio silence is what happened. The whole guard shift went on without a word with me just building up anxiety about it. After guard duty was over, I was called into my platoon sergeant's room, where he explained that he had to write a report about my negligent discharge. He had to send it up the chain of command and he did not know what would happen to me. I signed his report with a knot in my throat. That evening the whole company retrained on every weapon system we had. I felt lower than the belly of a snake. I was completely ashamed and I'm pretty sure everyone was angry with me. The military sure believes in its corporate punishment. After retraining on all the weapon systems again, I started to feel a little bit confident again on the .50-cal. When we switched missions with Second Platoon the following week, I was placed on the platoon sergeant's truck, which had a .50-cal. mounted on it for the mission. I immediately had an anxiety attack and told Sgt. First Class Savage I couldn't do it, and I didn't want to do it. He wasn't hearing any of that, because that's where he wanted me. We went on mission and ended up at FOB Brassfield-Mora. We unloaded our weapons per standard operation procedure (SOP), for safety. We got our supplies and mounted back up, and when I went to reload the .50 cal., I realized that a single round was still in the firing chamber. I could not get it to fall out, so I became gripped with fear and told Sgt. First Class Savage I did not want to be there on that weapon. Lt. Yoshio cleared the weapon for me, and I was again told to stay on the .50-cal. After getting back to PB Razor, I unloaded the .50-cal. again, and this time finally realized that the .50-cal. does not let go of that last round. It is designed to hold onto that last round and it doesn't always just fall out. You must physically take the round out with your hand or another object to truly clear that weapon. No one ever showed me that during training. This whole thing could've been avoided if I was trained properly.

One day the first sergeant called a formation to voice his frustrations about how all the toilet seats were getting broken and crapped on in the outhouses. He wanted it to stop because he only had a few seats left to replace those with. I thought this was weird and foolish, but a few days later we all found out how it was happening. A soldier spied on some others using the outhouses and found that one of our native interpreters was the culprit. You see, most of the country lived with little or no modern conveniences. His notion of a bathroom consisted of an open-air hole in the ground that he would squat over to do his business. So that's what he did, he stood on the toilet seats and squatted, thereby breaking the seats and crapping on them. If that wasn't enough, he did not use toilet paper, and even worse, he did not wash his hands. And the real kicker, this interpreter was then seen going into the dining area and grabbing some frozen chicken and pizzas to warm up in the microwave. These mini pizzas and precooked chicken pieces were in large plastic bags where they were all touching each other. I never ate any of the loose food items again that could be accidentally touched by another person.

Sleep deprivation was kind of a way of life, especially if you were on *missions* week and you had the lucky assignment of being at guard post R3 which was the guard post at the intersection of the Huiesh cut and Route 1. You would be there with your squad in one truck on top of a man-made sand pile surrounded by some sharp concertina wire and left there for about twenty-four hours at the least, depending on the mission. You might get dropped off more water and fuel to keep the air-conditioning in the truck going and maybe some MREs, or ready to eat, prepackaged meals, but that's it. Whenever we went out there, I just did not sleep—neither during the day nor at night. You were just flapping in the breeze out there. If anything happened there was not enough time for anyone to come to your rescue, so you had to be vigilant, so I did not sleep. One of these times I was the acting squad leader and we had been there probably two or three days. It was nighttime and to prevent all of us falling asleep we had to do a radio check every hour on the hour. The SOP became two people being awake at all times, because at some point one of the other squads had been found all asleep and they couldn't be reached over the radio. Anyway, it was night time, we had been there a few days, and I accidentally fell asleep. Then suddenly someone yelled, *"Let's go!"* Everyone who had been sleeping was shocked awake. They began running around making sure all of their correct gear was on and snapped into high alert for possible enemy activity. When everyone had gotten control of themselves, they looked over at me. There I was, fast asleep. Someone got up enough courage to wake me up and find out what was going on. As soon as they woke me up, I started screaming at them that they knew that I never slept out there and now that I fell asleep they had to wake me up! After I stopped yelling everyone looked at me dumbfounded and told me that I had yelled at them earlier, *"Let's Go!"* We all had a good laugh. At that point, we were all truly fully awake. You just had to be there!

Another long few days came in a similar fashion. My squad and I had been built up again and I was no longer squad leader. We had been out on R3 for a few days again when, in the middle of the night, the platoon came to get us for a night raid. So, we busted down a few doors in the area we were assigned to near Huiesh until we found a guy who was supposedly the brother of one of the top ten most wanted people at the time. After detaining him I believe we took him to the holding center nearby for questioning, and then it was pretty much daytime after that. We intended to drive back to base to get some sleep, but instead we were rerouted to check out a possible IED on the other side of Qulah. Sure enough, there was one there. We waited for EOD to come and blow it up like good little obedient boys. By this time, it was nearing lunchtime and we were all dead-tired. We mounted up again and headed toward base, but as a last task we were

*Depiction of my shooting incident in Qulah, Iraq in late 2005.*
*Original artwork by Nathan J. Gould.*

told to check the gas prices at the nearby gas station. The gas station happened to be in the center of Qulah. It was nearing the height of the day when people were everywhere, doing daily tasks like eating lunch and selling produce. I was on the turret-mounted 240B machine gun that day on Second Squad's vehicle, which was taking up rear security of the convoy. At first there was an IP vehicle directing traffic to go around our convoy about 3000 yards behind us, up over a small hill near a curve in the road that we could not see beyond. After about ten to fifteen minutes, the IP vehicle drove off and a few minutes after that a small white pick-up truck came barreling around the curve over that little hill directly toward us. There was one man in the vehicle who appeared to be white-knuckling his steering wheel staring straight forward, not even looking at me. He was not slowing down and then in my desperation I sprung up from my seated position waving my arms and yelling at the top of my lungs, "Oh-guff! Oh-guff!" which is how we pronounced the Arabic word for stop. He did not stop. Suddenly I heard gunfire on my left side, and I looked down and saw Sgt. Chavez firing his M4 at the vehicle. Then S.Sgt. Johnson behind him flipped around mechanically and did the same thing—all the while our driver Pvt. Owens was fearfully screaming. At that very moment, everything became like an out of body experience for me and my comprehension went into slow-motion. At the same time my vision seemed to go blurry. Apparently, I sat down in the turret, took aim, fired two bursts of three to five rounds, looked up, then remembered to fire a third burst, took aim again and fired one last burst of three to five rounds. Then I looked up again and the vehicle began to slow down with a slight turn to my left. I regained my focus and I looked at the driver as his car slowed to a stop about a hundred yards away. The driver began to sway in his seat and then he slumped over toward the passenger side of vehicle. I knew he was dead. Our medic ran to his aid, but it was too late. There was a straight line of bullet holes up the hood of the vehicle, then about a five-inch circular hole in the windshield and the guy's chest was red. I was in shock for a few seconds until S.Sgt. Bell came up and told me to snap out of it and to continue to look for threats. As we continued to sit there in the middle of Qulah, there were about a hundred people around. No one even ran away in fear. They stood there for a moment staring at us, and then they continued to do whatever they were doing before. It was like nothing had fazed them. In the next few minutes, a white van pulled up, grabbed the deceased person from the vehicle, put him in the back of the van and drove away. Then a few Iraqi men pushed the bullet-riddled vehicle out of the street and that was that. Shortly after that we drove back to base, finally. Then my squad had to go and talk to the first sergeant about what had just happened, which the Army calls an after-action review (AAR). I was so damned tired; I couldn't think anymore. I just wanted to get off my gear and go to sleep, because another mission was coming that evening, like it always did. I wanted to be left alone. No one really said anything and neither did I. I could tell the first sergeant really wanted to talk but, once again, we were in no psychological state to have a good conversation. So, we were released to go back to our containerized housing units (CHU) and get some much-needed rest. When it was just our squad in my CHU together, we actually did talk a little bit about the incident. I remember distinctly saying, "I got one more." I felt nothing. No remorse about having just killed someone. I did not feel bad; I did not feel good; I felt nothing. But my response of, "I got one more" meant that I was keeping score and I did not realize my thinking was skewed. I was lucky S.Sgt. Johnson, our new squad leader, was there and he challenged my thinking. I don't remember exactly what he said but he got me off the edge of my, *eye for an eye* mentality.

# CHAPTER 9: THE COLD SHOULDER

**AFTER I GOT SOME REST** I was thinking more clearly, so I decided to go talk with the first sergeant about the shooting incident I had just been involved in. I went looking for him and found that he was in his room. I knocked on his door and told him who I was and that I would like to talk to him, and for some reason he told me through the door that he was busy. I walked away and we never had that conversation. Although I started to feel like the first sergeant didn't like me, I am not sure that his not talking to me was intentional at that time.

In another instance, I began to become suspicious of the first sergeant's dislike toward me again when I came in from a daytime mission into our dining area with at least two other soldiers. He was right there and blurted out directly to me that I looked like I had just fucked his sister. He had a look of seriousness on his face and I couldn't tell if he was joking or not. I was speechless, and we just stood there staring at each other for a moment and then we walked in different directions. I went back to my CHU and took my gear off, and I have no idea where he went.

Later on in the deployment, things were going as smoothly as they could. Stuff became routine and seemed like clockwork. Gunfire at all times of the day didn't faze anybody, mortar attacks and rockets at night didn't wake us up. In fact, if I fell asleep, I was as good as dead to the world. During one of these times when I fell asleep, the Golden Mosque, which was a part of Samarra's skyline, was blown up in the middle of the night. I slept damned good that night and had no clue that had happened. The mosque was less than five miles away (see article link for Golden Mosque).

This next bit of information may seem trivial but, believe me, every little stupid thing contributes to PTSD. So here goes: one of those weeks that First Platoon was on guard duty and I had some free time, I decided to wash my clothes, doing it myself for the very first time, in one of our third world washers. I don't recommend this. Just pay the quartermaster, who is in charge of clothing and subsistence, to do it for you and quash the hassle. Lo and behold, as I walked into the laundry room, I ran into the first sergeant, who was doing his clothes in one of the washers at that time. At first, I thought of turning around and walking back out to avoid him, but instead I decided to stand my ground and wash my clothes in silence. But that was not to be. As soon as the first sergeant saw that it was me, he turned to me and accused one of my soldiers of breaking one of the washers by overloading it with clothes. I lost my cool. I forgot exactly what I said, but I know I yelled at him. I was so angry. I don't know what came over me, I yelled something in anger at him and immediately knew I had overstepped my rank. I began to backpedal, still seething with anger, and I said I would go get my squad right now; even though we did not know how to fix a washer, we would take it apart and fix it no matter what it took. Then the first sergeant, seeming to know that he stepped across an invisible line, said that was not necessary and he would leave then so that I could wash my clothes. After a minute or so, when he was out of sight, I also left the laundry room without doing my laundry and I never went back.

I paid for my laundry to be done by the quartermaster from then on.

Later on, after I was long out of the Army, as I began to reminisce about why it seemed the first sergeant would have such a weird vendetta against me and my guys, I thought maybe it was because

*Left rear armored door of Humvee 1-2, where I graffitied the word Father. This is also the place where I would have sat if I were in this Humvee. Years later I learned that Weiss actually sat there on that fateful day.*

he blamed me for Pauley and Weiss' deaths. Then I remembered something weird that happened after the incident at FOB Summerall. The wrecker vehicle had towed our mangled Humvee back to where we were staying at the time and parked what was left of it nearby our lodgings. I went out to inspect the damaged vehicle myself after the accident and found damages that seemed impossible physically to do to a vehicle that had about an inch of thick, steel armored plating on it. I inspected the door that I had inscribed/graffitied the word *father* on. If I were in the vehicle that day, that's where I would have been sitting. While I was standing there, the first sergeant walked up and asked me who had graffitied the door of the Humvee and I told him I had done it. I don't remember what he said, but he was not pleased.

I explained that I had seen others in the company doing something similar and I thought it was fine at the time to do. Shortly after that, the whole Third Brigade Rakkasans had red Toriis, Japanese symbol used in their unit, stenciled to the doors of their vehicles. I did not realize it at this time, but I began to believe and convince myself that the first sergeant had blamed me for the deaths of Pauley and Weiss from the very beginning.

During our stay at PB Razor there were a few stray dogs that accompanied us on base. There was a male dog that we lovingly named *Sapper*. He became somewhat of a mascot for us, and he trotted to and fro on and off base day and night with freedom I wish I had. He was a thin thread of hope I did not realize I had become tethered to. At some point our command was given use of a bomb-dog and his handler. After going on several route-clearing missions with us over a few weeks, they seemed to become one of the new permanent attachments that would be with us for the remainder of the deployment. But one afternoon as I sat in my CHU, I heard a single gunshot right outside my CHU door. I ran outside to see the source of the noise and found Sapper lying on the ground in the dust breathing his last breaths with a bullet hole in his chest as his blood trickled through the sand. I looked up in shock as the bomb-dog handler and his dog slowly walked away. Soon after that incident, the bomb-dog handler was sent back to higher command. Within the week the rest of the stray dogs, including puppies, were all put to death by our unit. The thought behind this, I think, was for some weird greater good and to take our minds off anything that may be distracting us from the mission at hand. For me, this was somewhat of a final blow for my morale.

Around this time, I became very depressed. I was sick of soldiering and I longed to live as freely as a *hodgie, which was an insulting term we had for local Iraqis.* I wanted to drop all my gear and become one of the blissfully ignorant. The end of our deployment was nearing, but it could not come quickly enough. All the days began to melt into one long day. It felt never-ending, and I stopped thinking about home. I felt trapped, like I was in a prison with no hope for escape or freedom. I lost track of time. I just stopped caring about it. I already was not eating or sleeping very much. You know you are at your lowest when the highlight of your day is volunteering to burn trash and fecal matter and getting excited about the warmth of the flames in the cold weather. I'm pretty sure I have pictures of me and a buddy with enormous grins on our faces! Wow, how sad that the moments I spent burning trash and fecal matter were about the happiest ones I spent over there. Crazy!

Toward the end of our time in Iraq, the brigade commander, Colonel Blood, traveled around to all the companies in his command after September 11, 2006 and personally handed out American flags

*Left: Sgt. N. Gould, Right: Spc. R. Booker on fecal matter burning duty at PB Razor.*

that had been flown over the Palace of Baghdad each for nine minutes and eleven seconds in remembrance of the September 11, 2001 terrorist attacks. He gave a speech with the whole company and handed flags out to every soldier after the speech. When it came down to our squad, he took the surviving members who were not injured or killed during the incident near FOB Summerall early in our deployment (Owens, Merrick, and me) aside to spend a few moments remembering our comrades with us. Especially given his position, this was a big gesture of respect and I honor him for that. But in the moment, all I felt was emptiness, empty gratitude. At the time, it meant nothing to me. At the time, I felt dishonored and disrespected. I cannot explain it, but the American flag felt like a disgrace in my hands; I was disgusted by it. I still tear up when I think about many of these things. This is how deep this crap gets to you, and as I'm writing this, that was fourteen years ago. Those feelings just hang onto you. You've got to let it out or it will destroy you.

# CHAPTER 10: R&R

**SOMETIME IN LATE MARCH 2006** I was scheduled to go on R&R back to the states. I was headed home to get rest and relaxation and a break from combat. It had been planned for me to go at this time because my first son was to be born sometime in mid-March. At this point in my deployment I was physically spent, emotionally drained, psychologically beat down, and I had lost a lot of weight from not eating or sleeping right. I had no emotions left to be happy about going home; I was expressionless. I could not tell anybody that I was coming home, just in case the message was intercepted by the enemy, but they knew around the time that I would be coming. I gathered my gear and started traveling toward Kuwait. We drove in Humvees, flew on Blackhawks and Chinooks, and finally got to Kuwait.

One important stop we made along the way was at Contingency Operating Base Speicher. It was a miniature USA in the middle of the desert. They had everything. I heard some soldiers had a nine-to-five working schedule, five days a week, with the weekends off. They had places you could get a haircut, tattoos, or a massage. They had movie theaters, gyms, and American-style houses with green lawns. I heard you could actually buy your own car to drive around on base. The place was humongous. You could get lost on this base. They had hanger-sized dining halls with chefs from the best restaurants that you could think of making you food. They had public transportation that would drive you anywhere you wanted for free. They had a fire department, police department, post office, and library. They wanted for nothing. It was as if they had never left America. I heard about guys that got DWIs and were thrown into the brig. I overheard a female soldier on my bus ride to the dining hall that was complaining about how her hair was dyed wrong and that she would have to go back tomorrow for them to fix it. I was disgusted by COB Speicher. Coming from a place where we lived like shit, ate like shit, were fired at daily, rocketed and mortared almost nightly, and every day we went out of the wire to dispose of IEDs and kick down doors, I was disgusted! I could not wait to get out of there. If this makes you mad as you read this next part, I don't care. Some of the soldiers at that base, and other bases just like it, were the definition of *pouges*, which was what we called the soldiers who stayed *in the rear with the gear* and don't do any of the fighting while deployed. How can you be living in that situation and get a combat action badge (CAB) when you never went outside of the wire for anything? The wire that I'm talking about for that base seemed to be about a mile from the outside wire to the inside wire. And then at least another mile or more to where people actually lived. Mortar attacks and rockets could barely reach that distance, if at all. You were in absolutely no danger. Disgusting. I really just wanted to throw up, literally. And it wasn't like a bad guy could walk right up to the outside wire for free and start shooting mortars or rockets. Both sets of wires (fences) were heavily guarded and patrolled. It wasn't going to happen there, period.

I finally left Kuwait on a commercial flight again back to Germany then back to the States. During this journey I found out about an awesome place at airports run by the United Service Organization (USO). These people really cared for soldiers. It was like a small taste of home in the middle of a busy airport, where you could hop in a bunk and get away from the hustle and bustle of the airport environment. The people there really cared for you individually. I felt at home, like my grandmother had cooked my favorite meal and she was there to wait on my every need—like I mattered! I hadn't felt that during the whole deployment, like I was something other than a piece on a chess board. On the other hand, I also sat alone at the airport waiting for my flight back to North Carolina and some well-meaning woman sat down next to me, took one look at the pitiful look on my face and said, "Cheer up, it's not so bad!" I don't blame her. How could she know?

I got back to Charlotte around dinner time on March 14. I called my wife to let her know I landed. The family came to get me, and we went out to Kobe Hibachi Steak House for dinner. We ate and relaxed with her family for a bit, and then we went home to our new house that I hadn't even seen yet. I went to bed with my very pregnant wife and we did what all married couples do when they haven't seen one another in six months . . . *sleep!* In a few short hours we were awakened by my wife experiencing very real labor pains. We headed to Presbyterian Hospital in Charlotte, where my first son Ethan John was born. I needed that miracle! Thank you, God, for caring about all the details! We stayed at the hospital for a few days and in the meantime my family from New York traveled down to spend whatever time they could with me. In those two weeks of R&R, I celebrated all the birthdays and holidays I missed or would miss in the next six months. I remember being welcomed back at church and thanked for my service and such, but the thought of having to go back there again was overwhelming. The weight of what had already happened was unbearable, but it was not the time to scare the hell out of my family with all that heavy shit. It was time to grin and bear it.

Two weeks went by too fast. I remember one of the first times I changed Ethan's diaper after we brought him home. I released the sticky tabs on the sides and the front flap flopped down, heavy with urine. As soon as that little guy felt the cool air, a golden stream shot out straight at my face. I dodged most of it as I had a Matthew McConaughey moment, *"Whoa! Whoa! Whoa! Whoa!"*

Before I knew it, I was back on a commercial flight headed to Iraq but this time I was quite desensitized, and I really started to care about only one thing: going home and bringing all my brothers-in-arms with me. I didn't really care about, *the mission*, or *winning hearts and minds,* that was bullshit. I hate to break it to you, but the majority of people were living in stone-age/bible-times conditions. They had all the third world problems we take for granted. Most were cattle herders. I would say some had to be farmers, but I never really saw any crops or much vegetation at all, unless it was directly adjacent to the rivers. It was a huge dustbowl wasteland. In general, the people only cared about their small nook of the world, which mostly consisted of a hardened clay house with a tin roof and a thick plate-metal front door. Some houses were better. You were either a *have* or a *have not*, there really was no middle class. I really only saw one place that was a rich man's house, the sheik of Huiesh. The outside of this large, two-story abode was not much to look at. It resembled the other houses in the area, earth colored and dull, but he had a golf-like lawn that was trimmed very low. When we went inside it felt like a museum where we shouldn't touch anything. The furnishings, walls, and ceilings seemed to be inlaid with real gold. It was like a small palace. We walked out to the back yard to speak with the sheik and found a well-manicured lawn and I'm pretty sure he had a fountain too. Other than the common look of the outside of the house, this place screamed extravagance. That building and all its inhabitants weren't stone-age mud-dwellers like the others; they had a modern life with modern conveniences. It really was a shock to see.

# CHAPTER 11: WINDING DOWN

**THE REMAINDER OF OUR TIME** in Iraq was kind of humdrum. Every other week was pretty much the same: wake up, go on patrol, and secure the route one week. The next week: guard duty and rest. Then repeat. During one of our missions weeks, my squad was on R3 guard post at the T intersection of the Huiesh-cut and Route 1. It was broad daylight, and I was on the turret watching the route when I observed an assassination. There was a white pick-up with one driver at the intersection in front of us. Then another pick-up truck pulled up behind it with two people standing in the bed wearing black head dresses that covered their faces while holding AK-47s. Without warning or any hesitation, the two people holding AK-47s lit up the driver of the other vehicle. They each basically unloaded their entire clip on this one defenseless dude. Then they drove away south on Route 1 toward FOB Brassfield-Mora. We called in the incident to command and they said they would come check it out. According to SOP we could not do anything about Iraqis killing

Iraqis, so we sat there watching the vehicle with the dead man in it. The strangest thing began to happen. The town of Huiesh was easily two to three miles away, and people began trickling in from all directions, walking to the location where this man had been shot. All of the people gathered at the vehicle, then some men took the body and placed him in another vehicle and drove away toward Huiesh and another man drove the shot-up vehicle away. Then all the people that had gathered walked back to where they came from and there was nothing left. From the time that we called in the incident to the time our mounted patrol came to check out the scene was only about thirty minutes, but now there was nothing left but shell casings in the dirt. It really was an awe-inspiring scene. It was like watching an ant hill ebb and flow flawlessly with so many moving pieces.

After that, we went to speak with the sheik of Huiesh and found out that it was his son who was assassinated by some other neighboring tribe vying for position in the hierarchy. It was a very brutal, savage way of forcing control onto others, and not civilized at all. That should give you some acute insight into the culture. Coalition forces would not be able to change this culture, ever. Why? Because we would be looked at in much the same way, just another tribe vying for total control. These people have been and are still living in a culture without structure and with constant leadership/dictatorship changes. Whoever had the power to overthrow who was in charge today could make new rules tomorrow—very, very unstable.

To win some favor with the sheik, we went on raids in Huiesh, nightly it seemed. Supposedly, during these raids one night we captured the brother of the number one or number two most-wanted guy from the coalition terrorist list at the time. We also arrested a man who had bomb-making materials in his possession. We went on a different raid with good intel and ended up killing two guys from the top ten most-wanted list, but the guy who we were looking for was not there.

One night an IA patrol had stopped on one of the bridges near us to inspect something suspicious in the roadway, which happened to be an IED. As they approached, it blew up. They frantically came to us, asking for help, and our guys went out and brought all of their soldiers back into our base. Two of them were already dead, and one was rushed into a makeshift surgery with our base doctor. It was basically medevac prep. Since we had a designated landing zone (LZ), we also dealt with medevac situations on a regular basis. This one guy was beyond the aid of our doctor and the only thing to really do was to bandage him up, give him pain medicine, and medevac him to a facility that could handle his injuries. The first sergeant hand-picked Sgt. Massy and I to help prepare this guy for medevac. We walked into the medical hut with the doctor and saw the bloodied-up IA soldier, who was continuously moaning and obviously already highly sedated. Both of his legs below the knee had been blown off as if he had been standing behind the open door of his vehicle on the bridge when the IED exploded in front of his vehicle. The doctor told Sgt. Massy and I to hold his legs up so he could wrap them with gauze for transport. The legs would not be saved, but they would be transported with the soldier. It really was a weird thing to behold. Both lower legs were only hanging by threads of elastic skin and the bones that I could see looked nothing like bone. They were more like bits of chopped up wood, split and shattered, but we held them while the doc wrapped them, and then we drove him off to the LZ, never to be seen again.

Before ending our time there, it was like the war movies where the soldiers you're rooting for have made it this far and they always have that last obstacle that will finally make or break them. Sometimes it's a necessary evil but sometimes it ruins the movie because a lovable character gets hurt, or worse, for no reason at all. During our last few weeks, a final mission was put together to go on a dismounted patrol into the bush near the river, across from where two roadside bombs had already been found previously on the other side of Qulah. One of those IEDs had actually killed a soldier in our battalion earlier in the year. It is a good idea to stop these IEDs, but not as much when the troops are beginning to think about home and losing focus on the mission. Command also decided it was okay for some troops to go on this final mission who hadn't gone on any missions at all the whole year long. I don't know how it happened, but both of those unexperienced soldiers who went on this final mission walked too close to an unseen IED and it went off. The shrapnel went straight up and got one in the face and only got the other one just a few nicks on his face and uniform. Getting shrapnel in the face got the one soldier hearing loss and partial blindness to one eye, a Purple Heart, and an early ticket home. I think the other soldier was so ashamed that it happened that I'm not sure he reported his injuries.

Shortly after that, a different 82nd Airborne unit was sent to take control of the base so we could leave. We showed them around for the next few days while they got acclimated to the environment. During this time, we patrolled and pulled guard duty together, and while doing this our company got orders for deployment to Afghanistan within the next eight months. My time of service was ending altogether, and the Army knew it. I was approached by my platoon sergeant, who offered me a squad leader position and E6 rank if I would enlist for another four years. I turned him down flat. I knew I was getting the hell out after I got back.

# CHAPTER 12: GOING HOME

**WE ALL PACKED TO LEAVE.** It seemed like forever before we finally left and drove to Brassfield-mora. Then we sat in the sand with all of our gear until dusk. Then a Chinook came to pick us up and flew us to COB Speicher. We stayed there two days or so and then flew on another Chinook to Ali-Al-Saleem in Kuwait. We spent about a week there until we finally got onto a commercial flight. It was pretty much the same trip to Iraq but in reverse, landing in Germany and then the US. That is when we were allowed to contact our families and tell them we were on our way to Fort Campbell. Landing back in the US was kind of amazing because I think the airline had announced to the airport that soldiers were coming back from war. We had a layover, so we sat in the concourse for a few hours and random people came up to us almost as we exited the ramp and offered us their cell phones to call anyone we wanted, for as long as we wanted or needed to. I can't explain how much that meant to me and the other guys. That small gesture, that small gift was one of the best I've ever received. It made me feel like America was really with us over there. Here I am crying about it again as I write this. Soldiers need to know you care!

No matter how small the gesture, it means a lot to that soldier, trust me! Thank you to all those who thank soldiers! You have no idea what they have been through.

After a few hours, we got back on another commercial flight and headed home to Fort Campbell. We landed on the tarmac and we were given orders before we even got off the plane. We were going to be exiting and marching straight into a formation. There would be a small reception speech of welcome while we stood at attention. After that we would be released to our families and the following day's formation would be at 8 a.m. After all that we would be released to our families. I was surprised that my six-month-old

September 3, 2006 Ft. Campbell homecoming celebration
captured by The Leaf Chronicle.

son eagerly hugged my neck and grabbed my ear and remembered who I was. I had feared that he may not know me. My wife, her parents, and their spouses were there to greet me. After a short reunion, my unit rushed quickly back to the company area to turn in our weapons to the armory. Then my family and I went out to dinner.

Reality soon set in: where was my family going to stay? A year before, as I packed for Iraq, my wife and I also packed up the house so she could move back to North Carolina to stay with her family while I was gone. We ended up buying a house and having a mortgage payment while I was in Iraq. This also meant we had no place at Ft. Campbell. I went to on-base housing to see if they had anything available and they did not, but they gave us several rental possibilities in the area that may help us with our situation. We signed a contract for six weeks in a duplex off-base.

The next day we were briefed in formation that we would be going through a ten day in-processing procedure. The only thing I really remember about those ten days was when our whole brigade was ushered into a large hanger for mass medical screening, bloodwork, shots, and the like. One side of the hanger was set up with a bunch of cots for us to wait our turn to get blood drawn, answer a questionnaire, etc. After that, we were given an opportunity to talk to a doctor about our war experiences on the other side of the hanger. Imagine a wide open-air hanger where everyone can see everyone else, everyone in the brigade was there. In front of the edge of the line of cots there was an ocean of pavement. Then a wall of white curtains hung, behind which there were doctors to talk to about our war experiences. It's set up so you go on a walk of shame to go talk to somebody about the negative experiences you may have had. I can tell you right now nobody in my company went over there, because that was for weak sissies. And probably the most important thing for us to do at that time was to go talk to a mental health doctor about our experiences. In fact, this was the only non-mandatory part of the whole ten-day decompression.

After those ten days were over, I was on a mission to get out of the military. My estimate termination of service (ETS) was coming up soon, even though I had been *stop-lossed*, where the military extended my service involuntarily, for about a month. I went through everything I had to do to get out. I was interested in law enforcement, so I planned on going to hear local personnel talk about their career. On that same day, Pauley's father showed up to the unit and Sgt. First Class Savage handpicked Merrick, Owens, and me to go have lunch with him. But I bowed out to go to the law enforcement informational meeting. Mr. Pauley I am so sorry I did not meet with you. I really wish I had met you so that I could tell you how proud I was of your son!

Within the next few weeks, I was getting my DD214, the official document that would officially discharge me from the Army, finalized and, because I had no work set up for me in North Carolina, I decided to enlist for one year of Army Reserves with the 108th in Charlotte. Then my family and I packed up and moved in with my mother-in-law and her new husband in Mooresville, North Carolina with our infant son in tow.

Here's some free advice about getting your DD214 *absolutely* correct before ETSing. *Do not* leave the Defense Enrollment Eligibility Reporting System (DEERS) office until they do it right! I left after telling them about one small change of the number five to the number six, with a promise that I would receive the corrected official copy in the mail within a month. Well, when I received my official copy it was not corrected. That seemingly small number change erased my deployment to Iraq, medals, citations, and awards I had earned. But more importantly, it erased a year of everything else in all other military systems and I began to get collection calls for a year's worth of health insurance bills and premiums I did not pay. I called the DEERS office that made the mistake and my unit for help. No one could do anything. I called St. Louis, where all military documentation is held, and got reamed out on the phone by some officer who said I didn't have authority to call them, the paperwork was right, and if I ever called again, I would have disciplinary action and probably lose rank. I never called again. It took over a year of snail-mail to get the corrections made. I learned another important lesson through this process: to the military you are only just another piece of equipment. While on active duty they lube you up, give you a wash when you're dirty, and always make sure your fuel tank is full and battle-ready. When you are other-than-active-duty, you are set aside, discarded, forgotten, or only get required yearly maintenance. And the maintenance is shoddy and half-assed.

# CHAPTER 13: YOU'RE OUT OF THE ARMY. NOW WHAT?

**WE MOVED IN WITH MY** mother-in-law, again! Come to find out, it costs money to move your pregnant wife back to North Carolina before being deployed. Then it costs additional funds to buy a house there and pay a mortgage. Someone has to pay for selling that same house and moving your wife and baby boy back to Ft. Campbell to live there in a rental duplex for a month and a half before packing it all back up again and moving back in with the in-laws. So, hazard pay, combat pay, and whatever monies earned while deployed were pretty much depleted and my wife and I felt like we were back at square one before joining the military in the first place. It was majorly discouraging.

I had trouble finding another job, mostly because I wasn't looking. I was really in a numbed-out state-of-mind and I needed a break, some real rest. Unfortunately, that's not how life works, right? So, I started carpet cleaning again with my wife's dad, except this time he was more established, and he found the jobs and I just did the work he provided.

During this time, I found I had a lot of time on my hands during the day and my new father-in-law had a full liquor cabinet. I had never been much of a drinker, not even in the military. I didn't even drink the *near-beer* available on deployment. But I found myself trying everything I could, just because it was there. And I did it every day—mid-day and night too. My wife began to get worried about my drinking and must have told our in-laws. Suddenly my daily habit stopped when I opened the cabinet one day, and it was bone dry. This just made me aggravated because I didn't have a *problem*, I was just using alcohol to help me relax and numb out. And they just took that away.

One day my wife and I took our son on a walk with the stroller. We were having a hard time learning to live together and relate to one another again. It was like we had learned to only depend on ourselves for the year I was deployed and now that I was home neither of us was willing to give that up or to trust each other. It felt like something had been lost between us. During the walk I struggled to bring up my worries about our relationship. I finally spilled the beans by saying, "I'm not going to do this, but my mind has been thinking we are headed toward divorce." As soon as I said that dreaded word, I watched my wife's whole demeanor and countenance shatter. I thought I had approached the subject with tact, but I had totally failed. Guys; never say the d-word. In fact, just own it and say something like, "I'm having trouble conveying my feelings. I need counseling and I would really like you to come with me." Anything is better than what I said. Because of that poor choice of verbiage, I had to show extra special loving gestures for the next week or so to get her out of the depressive state I sent her in at the mere mention of that word.

# CHAPTER 14: JOINING THE POLICE DEPARTMENT

**SOON I BEGAN LOOKING FOR** work again. Depressingly, I filed for unemployment thinking I could make a little headway while I did odd jobs here and there, but unemployment is not designed to be a way out. If I made more than five or six hundred dollars in a two-week period, I could not claim unemployment. So that was a dead end. I started filling out an application to join the FBI, but I got halfway through the preliminary online application and found that I would have to be willing to work weekends and holidays and immediately stopped filling it out. That was not for me. But as fate would have it, my brother-in-law called me up one day and suggested that I give law enforcement a try. He gave me the number of a recruiter. I called immediately, and the recruiter asked me why I waited to call. I said I just heard about it and he said to show up to the academy the next day for a physical assessment. I passed that test and they gave me an application packet to fill out. Talk about putting your life on paper! That took a while to fill out. Then there was a written exam, interview, polygraph, and a full physical exam before being accepted into the academy.

Within a few weeks I started the police academy and began to receive a steady check. The whole time at the academy I wasn't sure if I really wanted to be a cop. Everything was a life-or-death scenario and tests every week were pass or fail with only one retake. I only failed the phonetic alphabet once for spelling Lincoln L-i-n-c-l-o-n and got it right on my second try.

The police academy was great training but nothing like the real thing. It really was a sad comparison to real policing. We did a whole bunch of various trainings, but it really boiled down to a very few things. Basically, if you were afraid to die, you should get out then. If you were afraid to get in a fight—and there would be plenty of physical confrontations— you should go home. If you didn't have any common sense (or what the legal system deems *reasonableness)*, they don't need you, and if you're not a team player, you should go find another team.

Of course, you had to be able to qualify with a pistol during the day and night. You were tased, OC sprayed (pepper spray), and CS gassed (tear gas). You had to pass rigorous driver training and be in top physical condition. You also had to fistfight several consecutive on-duty officers and those guys were often mixed martial arts specialists or boxers. I had the pleasure of fighting the biggest guy there one day who kept front kicking me to keep me at bay. Then I went against a boxer who toyed with me and then finished me off with five or six body blows to my abdomen. He could have easily given me an uppercut and I would have been out cold, but he stopped. Then I had to grapple with another guy and we kind of got to a stalemate. Lastly, I faced an uncooperative person who I was supposed to handcuff, but he wouldn't give me his hands. So goes the police academy saying: *Ask them, tell them, make them.* I got the handcuffs on him.

*CMPD Police Academy graduation day 2007. Left to right:*
*Ethan, Nathan, and Rianne Gould.*

During this time my family and I moved into our own place. We began to get back on our feet again and our lives began to get some traction. Thank God, we found a little bit of stress release.

# CHAPTER 15: POLICE YOURSELF

**WITHOUT EVEN KNOWING IF I** really wanted to do it, I became a police officer. For a few months I was a trainee officer in what they call police training officer (PTO) phase. I was only shown the very basics and then suddenly I was on the street driving around in a patrol car enforcing the law. I rode along with a training officer on second shift and then two more training officers on the first shift. We did traffic stops, arrested some bad guys and girls, directed traffic, and did lots of accident reports—and computerized reports in general. Too soon I was on my own on third shift from 10:00 p.m. to 6:00 a.m. This is when the real training began. I learned a lot from mistakes and from other officers on my shift. Our command thought that more presence on the streets reduced crime. The idea was that the more often you see law enforcement the less opportunity you would have to commit or even think about crime. To accomplish this increase in police presence, there would be one officer per vehicle. This was all nice on paper but was very lonely. Even though you work for ten hours straight with ten plus other people, you barely ever see any of them, which limits opportunities for camaraderie to build. We would go to calls for service together and eat together if we could but that would be mostly business. This aspect of the job became very daunting to me over time. And I began to yearn for a partner to share the weight of the job with me.

I came into the job fresh, with some optimism. But the culture of policing is very negative in nature. You're always looking for bad guys, dealing with bad guys, meeting people for the first time on the worst day of their lives, and no one ever really liked seeing you. Policing is tough. Once in roll call, Sgt. Jim Frank said that you had to be a type A personality to be in law enforcement, meaning that you were a *take the bull by the horns* type of person. I remember thinking, *that's not who I am*! I have always been introverted, and this job challenged the core of who I was. I was never a go-getter or outspoken or had to have my voice heard. I would've rather faded into the background, but you just couldn't do that in this job and last. You had to be very assertive, sure of yourself, confident in your understanding of the law, and knowledgeable about a plethora of circumstances and instances. You had to pull it out of your butt at a moment's notice because people expected you to know. Your reactions depended only on what the bad guy did. If you did too much or too little you would be reamed out administratively. There might even be disciplinary action on you, affecting your pay, your job, or even land you in a pair of handcuffs if you did the wrong thing. Maybe you acted with too much force or not enough force? Everything was Monday-morning-quarterbacked. The weight of this job became very heavy, very quickly and with only two or three years in I was wondering how the hell I could get out. I felt trapped.

The *hero to zero* concept is very real in law enforcement, kind of like every superhero movie ever made. The good guys always play by the rules that no one else seems to have to care about. Here are a few examples of what I mean. An officer I know was on patrol one night when a fellow officer called for backup on a traffic stop. The officer I know was close by in his patrol car, so he turned around and sped up to go help out his fellow officer. Unfortunately, he never made it there. As he rushed to his buddy's aid, a car pulled out in front of him from a side street and he T-boned that vehicle, instantly killing one of the occupants. That officer's career and reputation was simultaneously over, and because he did not follow safety guidelines to the letter, he was hung out to dry and faced involuntary manslaughter charges all alone. Things like this seemed to happen quite often (see article link for Officer Proctor).

I had my own small taste of this one night right after roll call. An officer made a traffic stop and called for backup because another car pulled up behind him while he was stopped. I was about two blocks away, so I radioed that I was en-route. I was currently at a red light facing the opposite direction, so I signaled left and maneuvered into the left middle lane while checking my mirrors. Then, when the light turned green, I signaled left again, checked my mirrors and looked over my shoulder. No one was in sight, so I began to move into that left lane before making a U-turn. A mid-size SUV sideswiped my patrol car, knocking off the left mirror and spotlight. I was in shock for a second but quickly turned on my blue lights and siren, which automatically activated my dashcam and microphone. The driver of the SUV immediately cut across all lanes of traffic and pulled over on the right shoulder of the road. I called in the accident, the location, the stop, and asked for backup. Since I was involved in the accident, I could not legally do any of the reports, so another officer had to do that, and the sergeant had to come out and document any officer-involved incident. When the sergeant arrived, he asked the other driver a few questions, and then he questioned me too. He questioned me in a suspiciously leading and accusatory way. His body language and tone let me know I was in trouble. As I remember, he didn't believe that I looked behind me or over my shoulder to see if the coast was clear or that when the other vehicle sideswiped the patrol car, that he drove up on the median in an attempt to avoid me. Anyway, the sergeant soon left. The other driver ended up being drunk and, although respectful at first, refused to comply with roadside tests. We took him to the hospital to draw blood instead, as was policy, and he wound up physically fighting me, another officer, and a nurse. After all that—right out of the gate, mind you—I was radioed by the sergeant to come see him in his office. There I learned that he had deemed my accident preventable, which basically means it was my fault. I disagreed, but I signed the stupid report anyway because it just wasn't worth getting in a pissing match over.

As law enforcement you are always put in harm's way. You step into violent, hairy, messy situations and try to work out the best possible solution. You are the first line of fixers in society. In my opinion, a law enforcement officer makes all of the tough decisions, does the hard work, and make mostly correct arrests. After that, in the judicial system, things can get quite muddied, from the jail nurse, to the magistrate, to attorneys and so on. The system is far from perfect. The court system is where I personally found shortcomings. I may have charged a person with five or six crimes where three of the offenses were felonies, but if that person pleaded guilty to the agreed upon felony (at least amongst the attorneys), all the rest of the charges would be dismissed as if they didn't happen. I called this practice a joke and a dog and pony show, but I also found this process necessary, because if I didn't charge someone with everything I could, there might be some loophole to get them off scot-free. Also beware if you had to go on the stand and testify for anything, you often could only answer yes and no questions. Your integrity was always tested, and the defense was quite masterful at twisting your words to make the public think your arrest or citation was unlawful. You were definitely in the hot seat. I hated court. And I can't stand lawyers who seem to purposely attempt to skewer an officer's reputation. In the justice system we are supposed to be working together to better society, even if you are a defense attorney! There were some attorneys

I highly respected even if I lost a case against them. Why? Because they treated me like another human being, with respect, not like an enemy to utterly destroy. Judges have a very hard job too. They often have piercing insight and cut right to the heart of an issue, exposing criminals at face value. But sometimes the system fails, and they are forced to let go of a known criminal even if they want to put the person away for life.

There was a training once that the whole department had to take part in. It was a virtual reality training called a firearms training simulator (FATS), where you and another officer went into a dark room and stood in front of a life-sized screen that played out a situation that would require a use of force. You wore everything you would on an actual day of work, but you exchanged your pistol magazine, your Taser cartridge, and your OC spray for ones that looked and felt the same but had wireless sensors to record all of your actions, non-actions, and response speed. It was really cool, high-tech training. Plus, if you went through the training, you were not allowed to discuss it with anyone who had not done it yet, so everyone's purest responses would be recorded. All the scenarios started you off with an image of a paused screen so you could have a look at the environment and people before you started. The instructor would give a short synopsis of the situation, which gave you a general idea of what to do. The very first scenario showed a normal-looking man in his twenties to thirties wearing construction-like clothing in an industrial environment with his back turned to you. I'm not sure what the scenario explanation was verbatim, but it was something very vague like, "You are called to a construction site for a disturbance, and the foreman has told you that he had to fire an employee and now the employee will not leave. It is your job to escort this employee off the premises. Are you ready?" A short countdown was displayed on the screen, and then it went live. The guy kept his back to us. We attempted to talk to him and get him to turn around. We started to ask to see his hands and suddenly, without a word, he turned around and charged straight at us from a distance of twenty or so feet. I pulled my Taser, and my fellow officer pulled his gun. I shot my Taser too late and the other officer missed when he fired his gun. The suspect reached us, and the scenario was over. The instructor froze the last screen of the recording where it showed the suspect holding what looked like a screwdriver in one of his raised hands. According to the scenario, one of us would have been seriously injured or dead and neither of us reacted quickly enough. How long did this scenario last you ask? Six seconds. Let that sink in. There were two other scenarios, one about a hostage situation and one with a man that had a bomb strapped to his chest, but that first one was the most important (see article link for FATS).

About two weeks after this training an officer in our department had to face that very situation for real. He shot and killed the charging suspect, just like the training dictated, but the suspect was unarmed. This officer was charged criminally, dragged through the mud by the media, had to publicly apologize, and after the trial was finally over (more than a year later), he was exonerated. But the damage was done. His career in law enforcement was over. His reputation was ruined. Department policies left him high and dry. Like I said, this type of crap happened all the time. It became very real to me that any day the same thing could happen to me (see article links for Officer Kerrick case).

Then came a micro-managing sergeant. He questioned everything I did, and I felt like I was under a microscope. I started to second-guess myself and lose my confidence. He even asked me if I had any confidence in the job at one point. The dude went out at night and stopped drunks and then gave them to me to do roadside tests and the rest of the real pain-in-the-butt work. One night I worked on something that kept me until way past quitting time and all I wanted to do was go home. On my way home I received a call from him that I did not answer. I even turned my phone all the way off so I could just go get some rest because I was due back on third shift at 10:00 p.m. Before the shift the next day, I was on my way home from something with my family and our van got a flat tire. I knew I was going to be late, so I called in to work to let them know. When I showed up, I was met by another sergeant who tried to be a mediator between me and the micromanaging sergeant, who I'll refer to as *Micro*. He attempted to explain how Micro was a new sergeant and that I should give him some slack. I said, "Bullshit, he should back off!" Later that evening another officer told me that Micro had yelled at all of them in roll call and threatened them with a negative entry to Internal Affairs if any of them ever stood him up in court again! Apparently, I had been so tired that I forgot I had court the next day and they couldn't reach me because my phone was off. It also just so happened that it really was one of his drunk driver cases that he should have never handed off in the first place!

After a while, I got used to all of my reports being rejected and all of my moves being questioned by that sergeant that I expected it. Sometime around the Fourth of July, when there were always calls about gunshots (fireworks), there was a call for a person with a gunshot wound to the head. My buddy and I and several others hurried to the scene using full lights and siren. Upon arrival some people pointed out a person lying in a pool of blood that was coming from their head. There was medical personnel and firemen, who also located the person about the same time I did. The policy is to render aid until someone more qualified takes over. All of them were more qualified, but none of them approached the person. I told the medic to render aid, but they said something to the fact that the person was dead and there was no point. They didn't touch the person so I thought I shouldn't either, to preserve the crime scene. I knew time of death was important to the investigation, so I radioed in the time of death, to which Micro radioed for me to cease and desist, and for another officer to take over. No problem. I wasn't interested in going into the train wreck of a situation that I did not create. When Micro arrived, he basically reamed me out in front of my fellow officers, the witnesses, and the acting shift commander for the whole city. I felt like I was back in basic training and muscle-memory kicked in. I stood at parade rest and stared straight through him, turning my ears off and numbing out in the process. The shift commander beckoned Micro aside and basically told him this was not the time or place for that (see article link for Hawa Gabiddon).

Command sergeants, lieutenants, captains, and the like came and went. I switched to the second shift after being involved in two one-car accidents on my way home from third shift. Plenty of times I woke up while driving home and I was veering into oncoming traffic. Thank God He saved me from those. I was lucky to just drive into the ditch twice, but the second time my car was totaled, it was time for a change. Second shift was way busier with barely any downtime and a lot of accident reports. We dealt with a lot of *the world owes me a living* type of people and others who thought they knew the law better than us. I met rapists, gang members, runaways, drunks, prostitutes, murderers, robbers, thieves, and the list goes on. I had females attempt to seduce me to get out of tickets and a few who stalked me on Facebook. It seemed the world was out to get me, take my dignity, and tarnish my character at every turn. And from seeing what other officers had been put through after making a small mistake or even being inaccurately accused, I knew I was flapping out in the breeze all by myself, waiting for my turn in the laundry machine of justice.

Around 2008 the housing market crashed, and my wife lost her job. In 2014 we filed for bankruptcy and lost our townhome. We moved into a rental a few towns away, and I never told my supervisors at work, who I did not trust, about my personal problems. I just suffered in silence. It was a very emotionally trying time. My job performance went way down. Fewer arrests and fewer tickets. They may say, "there is no quota," but everything is tracked, totaled, compared, and made into percentages. During all of the years after getting back from Iraq my seasonal depression steadily became worse and everything else that was happening certainly didn't help. One day, after I had been depressed for three weeks straight and I could only just do the bare essentials of living, I made the kids lunches and drove them to school. I kissed my wife goodbye, and she went to work. There I was, alone, which is the worst time for any depressed person. I knew I had to go to training at the range and then to work afterward. The thought was overwhelming. I tried to escape these thoughts by turning on the TV, but I restlessly surveyed my watch every few minutes right up until I had to get ready to go. Then I jumped in and out of the shower and as I stood at my bed about to put on my uniform my eyes scanned over my gun and I thought about killing myself. But just as quickly I remembered all of the death investigations that I had been to and the unsuspecting family members that had found their loved ones who had committed suicide.

*Fictional image of the day I chose not to kill myself. This is my real bedroom and we really have that Love Life pillow on our bed. Those are my hands holding a gun that I own.*

I did not want my family to discover that I had done this, and to endure all the pain and endless unanswerable questions that would come with it. I became very afraid. I put my uniform on as fast as I could and started driving to the gun range for training. I noticed as I drove that I had a very dry mouth, and no matter how much water I drank, I could not quench the dryness in my mouth. At the training I could barely focus during the instructional phase. During live fire we had to mimic being shot in our dominant arm so that it was unusable and do everything with the opposite arm. Load, reload, clear a malfunction, and change a magazine with one arm. I remember feeling lightheaded at one point and my knees almost buckled. Then we cleaned our weapons and I prepared to go out on patrol. I got into my patrol car and began to sign on when a fuzzy tingling sensation began to start in my hands. I thought this was weird and decided not to sign on just yet. I started driving toward my division office and when I got there, the sensation had spread all the way up both arms. I thought, "I'll just sit here, give it a few moments, and it will pass. Then I'll sign on." The sensation spread to my chest and I began have tunnel vision and to sweat. I thought I needed help, so I telephoned my sergeant. As soon as I started telling him there was something wrong with me and where I was, I realized my words were slurring out of my mouth. Soon officers from the station came running out to my aid. They loosened my clothing and noticed I was sweating, white-knuckling the steering wheel, and had a rapid heartbeat. They secured my firearm before I was taken by ambulance to the nearest ER. Officers called my wife and doctors did tests. They said, "There's nothing wrong with you. All your vitals are fine. You can go home, and I'll prescribe you a day off." They asked me if I had thoughts of suicide and I said no because I was all too familiar with what happens to someone who admits that. They get sent to the mental health facility for ten days and then they're kicked to the curb with meds and not so much as a *have a nice life*. Nope, I wasn't going to admit that. I told the doctor, while blubbering, about friends who were killed in Iraq. He said I probably had survivor's guilt and something to the fact that it would pass in time. I went home utterly crushed and defeated.

I woke up the next two days with extreme anxiety about going back to work, about being a dad, and about stuff I didn't even know that I was thinking and dreaming about. I decided I needed help (see police and veteran suicide prevention information at the end of the book).

# CHAPTER 16: SEEKING HELP

**ON THE THIRD DAY, I** called in sick to work. I was having anxiety about anxiety. I felt I could no longer do the job. I was completely emotionally, physically, and psychologically drained. I had nothing left to give. I was broken and scared to death. I felt I couldn't do the simplest task. My wife was so afraid that she changed the code on our gun safe and hid all the bullets. I had already had a bad experience with the United States Department of Veterans Affairs (VA) in the past, but I knew I needed to try again. First, I went to my civilian doctor, who was infamous for just shrugging stuff off, so I chose another doctor in the same office and saw him for the first time. Although I felt like he took me completely seriously, he diagnosed that I was probably bipolar because I told him about my family history. He immediately gave me a prescription and free samples from his office and sent me home. I wanted a second opinion, so I scheduled an appointment with my VA primary care, and after that, a mental health appointment through the VA. After being interviewed by a mental health intake officer, I joined a group therapy session at the VA and also started seeing a civilian Christian counselor too. I was going to fix this, no matter what. I started going to two different men's groups from my church at this time as well. I did not go back to work for three months, until my confidence began to build up again. When I went back, they put me on a nine-to-five desk day job at the law enforcement center (LEC) in the financial crimes division. At first it was great! I wished I could just stay there and still do my part. I cranked out more financial crimes reports than you would believe. But even that became overwhelming, and some days I felt the walls of my cubicle begin to gobble me up. During this time, I was on a temporary light-duty status and did not have any control over sensitive equipment like my gun, Taser, OC spray or police radio anymore. I had no law enforcement authority and that was perfectly fine with me! Around the six-month mark of my incident, I was commanded to get a third-party evaluation of my mental health. I filled out several bubble exams, wrote essays, and was interviewed extensively. But it seemed the real test was just one question. Do I feel ready or am I ready to go back to patrol? I said I did not know. Return to full duty status, *denied.* After another three months I went through the same process again, but with the head psychologist. When asked if I was ready, I said I did not feel safe to go back and possibly put myself or my fellow officers in danger. I said no. In a week or so, the day before my birthday, I was called up to human resources and advised of my second not-fit-for-duty evaluation and then I was given a few choices. First, I could no longer be a sworn officer and the job openings they had right then were animal control and communications/dispatch. I could also choose to just cut all ties and my career would be over that day. I could file for disability, or I could choose nothing and the choice of being cut off would be made for me. Of course, it sounded more flowery than that, but that's the gist. I chose to file for disability, as I had planned to do that for several months if it ever came to this.

Originally, I was awarded disability, but the paperwork plainly said that I might have to prove my disability status each year to make certain conditions of my disability remained. A year rolled around, and I went to my civilian counselor, who filled out my original approved state disability paperwork and asked her to fill it out again. She did, but this time it was denied because the premises for approval was PTSD. I did not have an official PTSD diagnosis, even though I had been going to VA mental health appointments religiously for a year and the doctors had told me that PTSD is what I was dealing with. I took the next step further and went to advanced psychotherapy through the VA specifically for PTSD which is a one-on-one session with a specialized VA therapist. I spent months reliving the most traumatic event in my deployment, when my fellow soldiers were killed. I tasted the sand and smelled the diesel fuel. I heard the dreaded machine gun fire that ended up being farm machinery. I saw the bloody white sheets over my buddies on gurneys being loaded into medevacs. I said the words, "we hear a machine gun firing over there," while pointing, that I radioed up the chain of command that fateful day over and over again into my recording machine to listen to again everyday as an assignment until our next session. I wept and shook again and again until I no longer did. I stopped being hypervigilant. I stopped fearing crowded spaces and thinking everyone was out to get me. I stopped believing I had caused my brothers to get hurt and die. I let go of my burdens. Is this hard work? Hell yes! Can you do it too? Hell, *yes, yes, yes*! Do I still get blindsided by overwhelming emotion at times and around certain seasons? Absolutely. But do I have tools to help me overcome these obstacles? I do now.

I will be a PTSD patient for the rest of my life. I take daily medications to help with extreme depression and to stabilize my mood. I have even decreased in dosage since the beginning. Guys, this mission is doable. You can do it too. You say you don't trust the VA, the system, or the man. They have all gotten a huge wake-up call in recent years, with the large numbers of wounded warriors that would have just died on the battlefields in the past now flooding the mental health systems. PTSD is real, and if we don't do something about it, it will literally kill us. You can look up the suicide numbers too and do the math (see suicide prevention information at the end of the book). I almost killed myself, I know. Note: I also wrote a letter to Pauley's parents and only sent it after writing this book, which I've included in the final chapters.

Anyway, I finally was diagnosed with PTSD. My state disability was approved. Now what was I to do with myself? Was the journey over? Was I just broke? Did anyone care? Was there any help with my new reality?

# CHAPTER 17: A NEW LIFE

**I DID NOT KNOW WHAT** to do with myself at first, so I did nothing. I became a stay-at-home-dad. My days were filled with housework, helping kids with homework, and taking kids to lessons, tutoring, and sports. I also did yard work and odd handyman-type jobs for family and friends.

Then one day I wrote a story about me and my family called, *Mr. Mom's 1st day of School.* I've always liked to write, and I decided to illustrate the story myself, in pencil at first. My wife has always been more of a techie, so naturally she wanted to get some sort of drawing program for me. We got me a huge iPad and Adobe Sketch, and after some playing around, I figured out how to do it. I poured my extra time into this endeavor and was roughly finished within three months. I joined CreateSpace (now Kindle Direct Publishing) to self-publish for cheap. My brother edited, formatted, and submitted the final product about a year later. It was a long process, but we learned a few things.

*Original drawings, digital drawings, and the finished children's book, Mr. Mom's*
*1st Day of School, by Nathan Gould.*

Writing this book has been its own therapeutic journey, for sure! I have written a letter to the parents of Anthony Pauley, the boy who was taken too soon and was truly like a son to me. It took me over ten years to write that letter and face his parents. They haven't written me back yet, but I hope to actually face them one day and then cry with them. This crap is the toughest thing I've ever done in my life! Facing my own faults, admitting I failed, being vulnerable, and opening my heart to others. I have even started to attempt to talk to my first sergeant, which is another conversation I have avoided for more than ten years. I also don't know how that relationship or conversation will end up because I'm dealing with it right now.

My point is: find something, anything, to pour your new you into. The US Marines say *Improvise, Adapt, and Overcome.* All service members have some sort of creed that adheres to this. Just apply whatever it is to your new you—your new life, your new reality. One day at a time, my friends, one day at a time.

**Matthew 6:25–34** (NIV)

**Do Not Worry**

25"Therefore I tell you, do not worry about your life, what you will eat or drink; or about your body, what you will wear. Is not life more than food, and the body more than clothes? 26Look at the birds of the air; they do not sow or reap or store away in barns, and yet your heavenly Father feeds them. Are you not much more valuable than they? 27Can any one of you by worrying add a single hour to your life?

28"And why do you worry about clothes? See how the flowers of the field grow. They do not labor or spin. 29Yet I tell you that not even Solomon in all his splendor was dressed like one of these. 30If that is how God clothes the grass of the field, which is here today and tomorrow is thrown into the fire, will he not much more clothe you—you of little faith? 31So do not worry, saying, *What shall we eat?* or *What shall we drink?* or *What shall we wear?* 32For the pagans run after all these things, and your heavenly Father knows that you need them. 33But seek first his kingdom and his righteousness, and all these things will be given to you as well. 34Therefore do not worry about tomorrow, for tomorrow will worry about itself. Each day has enough trouble of its own."

# CHAPTER 18: EPILOGUE OF ENCOURAGEMENT

**SINCE BEING DIAGNOSED WITH PTSD,** I really have been freed from a huge burden I've been developing and carrying for over a decade. I now have written, illustrated, and self-published two children's books. I'm almost finished with my third book and have started the fourth. I am finishing this book, which you are now reading. I never intended on becoming a writer or author, it was just the next thing that came to me. Whatever you do, just keep moving. Put one foot in front of the other and one sock on at a time. Before you know it, you will be at your next destination embarking on the next mission, full steam ahead. Find your purpose again. You can do it! You are worth it and your journey matters! Your family needs you to take courage and charge back into the fight. Win at your own life, because this is the only one you'll get. If you journey down this road on this greatest marathon, you will cross the finish line and join the ranks of the courageous few who come out the other end of the rabbit hole into Wonderland. Share your story with another service member and see that you're not alone. Find camaraderie again. You are worth it! I love you and safe travels!

May God bless you and keep you, and may His face shine upon you, and give you peace. Amen (Numbers 6:24-26, paraphrased).

# LETTER TO PAULEY'S PARENTS:

Dear Mr. and Mrs. Pauley,

Hello, my name is Nathan Gould. I was one of your son Anthony's sergeants during the time he spent in Iraq. I would like to say that I am sorry for your loss. I have been meaning to reach out to you for some time. Please forgive me for my delay.

I want to share a story about Anthony with you that was a true wonder of transformation that occurred in his life. When Anthony came to our unit in early 2005, he did not have an easy time. At one point he was not sure if he wanted to stay in our unit or reclassify into another MOS.

Just before we deployed to Iraq was a hard time of constant intense training because we knew we were leaving in September. The reclassification option was going nowhere, and then in June we went to Ft. Knox for a month-long firearms training, where we learned to move and shoot as a group. We were on the line from sunrise to sunset, nighttime, and any time we could get our hands on more bullets. There came a point when Anthony was discouraged and he wanted to stop training, so he was allowed to have a break by my squad leader. During this time, I went to speak with the first sergeant about Anthony. In short, the first sergeant said to me that no one is going anywhere. We are all going to Iraq together. He also told me I could no longer be easy on Anthony. In fact, I actually had to be hard on him from now on. I did not want to do this, but I obeyed. I went back to Anthony and told him exactly what the first sergeant told me. At this point I believe Anthony started to accept that he was staying in the unit with the rest of us.

After Ft. Knox, and the new way of soldiering Anthony, I began to see an awesome change in Anthony. His confidence was growing. He believed in himself. It was one of the greatest transformations I have ever witnessed! I was very, very proud of the man he was becoming. I remember telling him to choke out the guy who used to haze him most every day and he attacked. He didn't win, but he didn't give up or lose his confidence and winning spirit. I remember his smile beaming from ear to ear when he did it. No one saw that coming. This is how I remember Anthony; he became like a son to me! I cared about him and loved him very much!

There is one last memory about our time in Iraq I would like to share. He and I were not assigned to the same truck during our missions. He was in Second Squad truck and I was placed in Third Squad truck. There came a time, after we had gone on a few missions while at FOB Summerall, that he approached me and told me that he did not think he could do what he had to do if it came down to him doing it. I put down what I was doing, and he and I went into the empty warehouse next to the one we were staying in. I stood in the middle of the empty warehouse and told him I was not going to fight him. I was not going to run, but I was going to walk through that front door. I said if he let me walk through that door then there would be hell to pay. I did not make it through the door.

That was the last thing I remember about Anthony. He was confident; he was ready; he was prepared to take on the world. I also believe he was ready and prepared to see Jesus. It is my sincere hope that I will see him again someday in heaven!

God Bless you!

# ABOUT THE AUTHOR:

Nathan Gould is a veteran of the United States Army, a retired police officer, a stay-at-home dad, and recent author of *Service to Civilian—A Journey Through PTSD*. He is an Iraq War veteran who retired from policing after having a PTSD episode while on duty. He has written poetry and short stories from a young age and has self-published two children's books: *Mr. Mom's First Day of School* and *A Mole Named Cole Dug A Hole*. Nathan loves Jesus, chess, CrossFit, a steaming hot mug of coffee, and making foot-in-his-mouth sarcastic remarks. He spends his days loving his three kids and wife in the great state of North Carolina with their Boxer-Pit mix, Cookie.

# ACKNOWLEDGMENTS

Special thanks first and foremost to my Lord and Savior, Jesus Christ, without whom I probably wouldn't be here right now! Thanks for having my back, battle buddy! You rock! Secondly, thanks to my talented, beautiful bride Rianne Gould for sticking with me through thick and thin, designing my author website and so much more! It's you and me babe, *Come What May* – Moulin Rouge. Next, thanks to my close family and friends who read this book before its release and gave me their honest feedback so that I could make its message even better and relatable to the reader. You guys know who you are. I love you with all my heart! XOXO Special thanks to Jeremy Scott, Jonathon Maloney, Brent Plott, Joshua and Sonya Miller, Angela Austin, Kenneth and Patti Silverman, Jess Christy, Jodi Newell, and Dana and Elise Parker, who donated to the publication of this book through my GoFundMe page for nothing in return. Thank you for your selflessness and monitory sacrifice, it matters. Lives will be changed by this message! Another special thanks to Raymond J. Gould, Ian Mackenzie, Dana and Elise Parker, Jesse Casler, Andy Foster, Jeff and Abigail Riggall, Adam and Lori Ziegler, Michael Hansen, Paul K. Tamer, Jonathan Ray Haul Gould, and Calvin and Lisa Stalnaker, all of whom pledged fifty or more dollars to my Kickstarter campaign. Rock on! To Koehler Books, thank you for partnering with me to fine-tune my story and champion it in such a way as to take ownership with me to bring the message of hope to the masses. Thanks also to Yulanda Langone from YDesign & Photography for bearing with me during the photo shoot. That was a hilariously great time!

# KU-WAIT

*By: Nathan Gould*
*September 4, 2005*

Life is at a pause
Every day is just like the last
We wake before the sun rises
We conduct all the same tasks

A year of life
Just like this from dawn till dusk
Dark o'clock until the same
The monotony is so lame

At least my smallpox
Shot is finally healing
Chess, cards, phones, Internet
Even training's better than staring at the ceiling

I've even started this poem
Just to keep myself busy
No one knows what's going on
They say, "When we get there we'll see."

So I wash my hands, brush my teeth, shave
And then go back to the tent
Where again I'll await another day
Until we get back from deployment

*Reading a book at R3 guard post with one of Sapper's pups.*

# NEWS ARTICLES

**Officer Kerrick Case**
https://www.charlotteobserver.com/news/local/article38223657.
html, https://www.charlottemagazine.com/lines-of-duty-chief-
rodney-monroe/, https://www.charlotteobserver.com/news/local/
crime/article30514749.html.

**Officer Proctor Case**
https://www.wbtv.com/story/10237170/cmpd-officer-charged-
with-involuntary-manslaughter/

**Golden Mosque Terrorist Attack**
https://time.com/2920692/iraq-isis-samarra-al-askari-mosque/

**Hawa Gabiddon Murder**
https://www.wsoctv.com/news/local/woman-found-shot-death-
woods-north-charlotte/329541190/

**Veteran Suicide Statistics**
https://allthatsinteresting.com/veteran-suicide

**FATS Article**
https://www.charlotteobserver.com/opinion/op-ed/
article19426401.html

**Police Suicide Statistics**
https://abcnews.go.com/Politics/record-number-us-police-officers-
died-suicide-2019/story?id=68031484

# SONGS THAT HELPED

**Going to Basic Training:**
Nicole Kidman and Ewan MacGregor. "Come What May." *Moulin Rouge* soundtrack.

**Iraq:**
3 Doors Down. "Here Without You."
Marc Schultz. "He Will Carry Me."

**Bankruptcy:**
Unspoken. "Lift My Life Up."
The Afters. "Broken Hallelujah."
Steven Curtis Chapman. "Long Way Home."
Tenth Avenue North. "Hold My Heart."

**PTSD attack:**
Toby Mac. "Move (Keep Walking)."

**Everyday living:**
K-LOVE radio network

# SUICIDE PREVENTION INFORMATION

**Nationwide Suicide Lifeline** – The Lifeline provides **24/7, free and confidential** support for people in distress, prevention, and crisis resources for you or your loved ones, and best practices for professionals. **1-800-273-TALK (8255).** https://suicidepreventionlifeline.org.

**Veterans Crisis Line** – Connect with the Veterans Crisis Line to reach **caring, qualified responders** with the Department of Veterans Affairs. Many of them are Veterans themselves. **1-800-273-TALK (8255) and Press 1 or TEXT: 838255, for deaf or hard of hearing 1-800-799-4889.** https://www.veteranscrisisline.net.

**Suicide Prevention Resources for First Responders** – The following programs will directly help you or help connect you to the resources you or a loved one needs. **1-800-273-TALK (8255) or TEXT: BADGE to 741741 https://www.sprc.org/settings/first-responders.**

# US ARMY UNITS

| | | |
|---|---|---|
| Field Army | 50K+<br>Soldiers | Commanded By:<br>★★★★<br>General |
| Corps | 2+<br>Divisions<br>20-45K Soldiers | Commanded By:<br>★★★<br>Lieutenant General |
| Division | 3<br>Brigades<br>10-15K Soldiers | Commanded By:<br>★★<br>Major General |
| Brigade/<br>Regiment | 3-5<br>Battalions<br>2-5K Soldiers | Commanded By:<br>★/ ✹<br>Brigadier General/<br>Colonel |
| Battalion | 3-5<br>Companies<br>100-1K Soldiers | Commanded By:<br>✹<br>Lieutenant Colonel |
| Company /<br>Battery / Troop | 3-4<br>Platoons<br>60-200 Soldiers | Commanded By:<br>▊ / ▊ / ✹<br>Captain / First<br>Lieutenant / Major |
| Platoon | 3-4<br>Squads<br>18-50 Soldiers | Commanded By:<br>▊<br>Second Lieutenant |
| Squad | 6-10<br>Soldiers | Commanded By:<br>⟪<br>Sergeant |

# MAPS

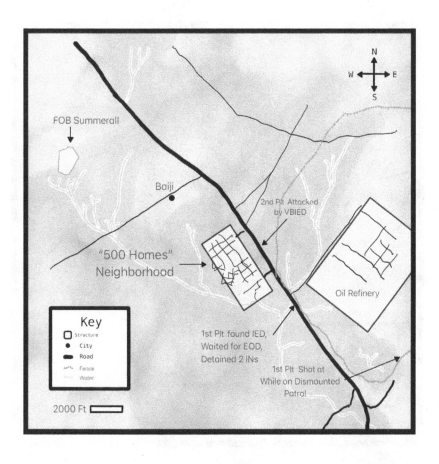

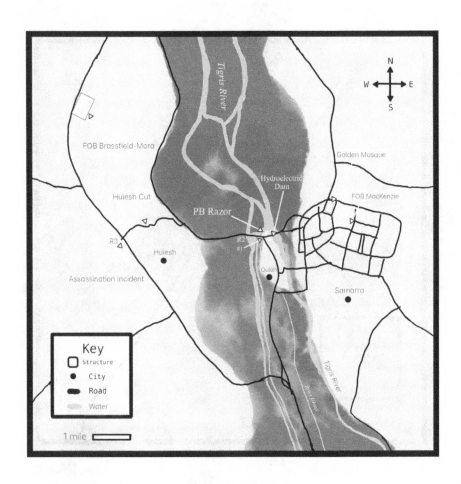

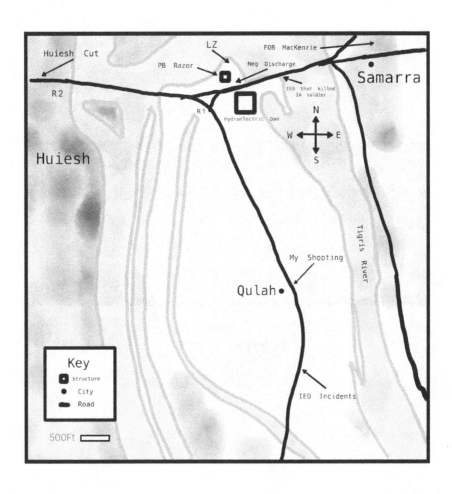

Huiesh Cut

LZ

FOB MacKenzie

PB Razor

Neg Discharge

Samarra

R2

IED that killed
IA soldier

R1

Hydroelectric Dam

N

W ←→ E

S

Huiesh

Tigris River

My Shooting

Qulah

Key

Structure
City
Road

IED Incidents

500Ft

*Balmy Iraqi sunset.*

CPSIA information can be obtained
at www.ICGtesting.com
Printed in the USA
LVHW032333210521
688193LV00006B/307